David P. Robbins

Descriptive Sketch of Winston-Salem

Its Advantages and Surroundings, Kernersville, etc.

David P. Robbins

Descriptive Sketch of Winston-Salem

Its Advantages and Surroundings, Kernersville, etc.

ISBN/EAN: 9783337193676

Printed in Europe, USA, Canada, Australia, Japan

Cover: Foto ©Andreas Hilbeck / pixelio.de

More available books at **www.hansebooks.com**

SINGLE COPIES,   50 CENTS EACH.

DESCRIPTIVE SKETCH

—OF—

WINSTON-SALEM,

ITS ADVANTAGES AND SURROUNDINGS,

KERNERSVILLE, ETC.

COMPILED UNDER AUSPICES OF THE

CHAMBER OF COMMERCE,

FROM A MATTER OF FACT STANDPOINT,

BY

D. P. ROBBINS, M. D.

WINSTON, N. C.:
SENTINEL JOB PRINT
1888.

☞ *The sender of this pamphlet calls your attention to pages........*

TABLE OF CONTENTS.

Banking Interests,...23
Churches,..16-17
Chamber of Commerce,............................97
Drugs and Paints,.................................76-77
Electric Light Company,..............................22
Forsyth County,...11
Fries, F. & H., Manufactories,..................24-5
Gun and Locksmiths,..............................54, 81
Groceries, Confectioneries, etc.,..............78-80
Hardware, Stoves, etc.,...........................75-76
Healthfulness and Salubrity,.........................5
Historical and Geographical,........................4
Hygiene in Brief,...65
Hotels, History, etc.,....................................45
Iron Working Interests,.................................26
Ice and Coal,..78
Jewelry Stores,..77
Kernersville,..84-93
Legal Fraternity,......................................49-51
Livery Stables,.......................................68, 95
Mercantile Interests,..................................70
Manufacturing Inducements,..............2, 7, 82
Moravian Church..15
Miscellaneous Manufacturing,..........30, 55, 80
Medical Profession,..............................51-53, 80
Merchant Tailoring,.....................................55
Millinery Stores,..78
Northern Capital Coming South,................2, 3
Newspapers, Job Printing, Etc.,............20, 21
Photograph Artists,....................................54
Public Schools,.......................................14-15
Post-offices,..21
Public Buildings and Officials,................46-49
Railroads....................................44, 66-68
Real Estate and Broker,..............................54
Salem Female Academy,..............................13
Salem Merchandise etc.,...........................69-70
Settlement of Salem,....................................9
Stokes County,..12
Societies,..18-19
The Twin-City,...10
Tobacco Interests,..................................31-44
Valuable Statistics,.................................57-64
Wagons, Carriages, etc.,..............................29
Winston Merchants,................................71-75
Wood Working Interests,..............................27

Winston-Salem, N. C.

Compiled under auspices of the
Chamber of Commerce.

The Leading Manufacturing and Mercantile Enterprises, Public Men, Schools, Churches, Railroads, Advantages and Surroundings Properly Portrayed.

In the following pages we shall not go into lengthy details of private enterprises or fulsome praise of individuals, but it is the purpose of the compiler and interested citizens of this place, to present in a convenient shape for preservation, and in as brief a manner as is consistent with an intelligible description of the facts, (yet withal so inexpensive and easily mailed as to be sent far and wide by the promoters of this section), a sketch of our advantages and surroundings, which shall show forth to the world the undoubted superiorities of our city and that our progressive men are ready to welcome any legitimate industry. A summary of these advantages will demonstrate to the reader that Winston and Salem are equalled by few cities in the South. Read the following pages and refer them to the manufacturer and capitalist, as well as to those who seek after health and comfort, beautiful surroundings, educational and social advantages.

It is not proposed to write much of our city's past history, however full it is of tender memories, of pleasing reminiscences, of high achievements, and of solid enterprises; however replete with the private heroism and the public heritage of noble men and saintly women, who have done their allotted parts and passed away to live only in their works that have not perished. The story of this glory is foreign to the purposes of this publication. Let the dead past bury its dead. Honoring it highly; cherishing it tenderly; accepting gratefully the lessons it teaches of moral and economical import—of ethics, education and business—let the record be laid aside. Let the present be grasped and so wisely wielded and worked that we may go forth to meet the shadowy future without fear and with a manly hope.

The purpose of this pamphlet is to exhibit in a condensed form, in logical order of arrangement, and with strict regard to the truth, the resources and advantages of this city and country as a place of residence and a business mart. The object is to show accurately its railroad resources, religious, educational, industrial; its banking and mercantile facilities; its hygienic advantages and general attractions, extenuating naught and setting down nothing in exaggeration of the facts of the case. No *boom*—fit word of recent usage to express exaggeration, false statements and fallacious reasoning, to come back like an Australian missile weapon, with inevitable reactionary force, is here designed; but on the contrary, with confidence even in such wounds as the truth gives to say nothing of the power that it ever carries, it is intended to give a plain, unvarnished exposition of our real condition and reasonable expectations. Fortunately for us, we have a cause that can stand upon its real merit—a case that is good in court—requiring no artful declarations, no labored plea, and no technical support.

MANUFACTURING INDUCEMENTS.

While the mercantile interests of a community are an essential feature and the professional talent a necessary part of a city, it is generally admitted that thriving manufacturing industries are the great *desideratum*, and give more permanency and rapidity of growth to any place than all other interests combined. The merchant brings to us the commodities of commerce and is usually generous in dividing his profits to charities and enterprises of public good, but the legitimate manufacturer opens a permanent investment for capital at remunerative rates, gives employment to the laborers of a community, and enhances the values of all farm products in his immediate section. The Twin City, with her coming railroads and healthy location, offers superior inducements to those who may desire to make investments within her borders. Lands are cheap, laborers plenty, educational advantages of high grade, her citizens noted for their culture, hospitality and generous welcome toward good citizens from other states or countries.

The growth of the South in a few years past has been wonderful, and this place is awakening to her importance as a central city. A Northern journal says: "The summary of industrial statistics, which has been made by a Southern trade journal, discloses a progress along the lines of diversified developement, which will be a surprise even to those who have fancied that they appreciated the changes which are in progress in that section. Twenty-two factories for making agricultural implements; 23 car works; 147 cotton and woolen mills; 184 foundries and machine shops; 73 blast furnaces; 504 mines and quarries and 23 rolling mills. These are a few items in a long list of industries begun or established during a single year in thirteen States." Such an industrial development as this, so rapid and so varied, shows the necessity of recognizing the new impulses and conditions which prevail in the South, and is changing the character, traditions and aspirations of the people of this section.

NORTHERN CAPITAL COMING SOUTH.

The statement given forth by Northern journals that one hundred and sixty millions of Northern capital has found investment in the South within the past year raises the question as to what particular industries have absorbed so large a sum in this section of the country. Undoubtedly a large amount has been employed in the construction and improvement of railways and the development of mining, milling and manufacturing interests, but it has been shown that considerable capital has also been used in a comparatively new direction. The cutting down of forests in the South by saw mill owners has opened up large tracts of land which are gradually being turned into farms. Much of this land, when fertilized, is capable of yielding as good crops of cotton, corn, fruits and vegetables as Western or Gulf State lands. The opportunity thus offered to secure homes in the South, where the climate permits out door work the year round, and where the rigors of a severe winter are escaped, has been seized upon by many small capitalists in the North and West. A number of well-to-do famers from Northern Ohio, tried the experiment in Southern Georgia last year, and their experience is said to have been very satisfactory.

It is becoming plain that the South must look to the farmers and mechanics of the North and West for the increase of its white industrial population. Immigrants from Europe cannot compete with the negro in unskilled labor and, therefore, will not go South for the present, failing to realize the vast advantages which this region offers agriculturally. Thus, to the Northern or Western man who has the means for investment, this new branch of small farming in the South offers inducements unequaled perhaps by those of any other country. Certainly the great Western States and Territories, great as their advantages undoubtedly are, offer no finer chances to men of small capital and enterprising purpose than the 'New South' presents. It is an encouraging fact that a considerable part of the capital which is now pouring into the South has found employment in the way we have indicated, contributing thus to the diversifications of Southern industries, and to the welfare of the country at large."

THE SOUTH INSTEAD OF THE WEST.

The stereotyped idea that the tide of immigration follows natural lines from East to West, has received a rude shock from the interest evinced by people in all parts of the world to know more of the vast mineral and agricultural resources of the Southern States, and it is now certain that a tide of immigration has commenced, which, although small at first, is steadily, healthily and rapidly increasing. It is now everywhere recognized that there are in the South, more and better opportunities for people of moderate means than in any other section of the United States, and it is not at all surprising that there is such an eager inquiry from all directions. Since 1880 the progress of Southern agricultural pursuits has been very great. This is explained by the fact of improved cultivation of the soil, diversification of crops, better labor, better yields. In 1880 the crops of the South were $612,278,318; in 1887 they had risen to $745,050,696; an increase of 22 per cent. Cotton is still the largest item, constituting one-third of the whole yield.

Fruit and garden crops have increased $13,000,000, and the value of stock $247,326,348, or 60 per cent.

The South's saw-mill and forest products establishments have increased in numbers 2,768; in hands employed, 27,597, and in value $22,582,137.

Including the farm, stock-raising, manufactures, minerals and fisheries, we find a grand aggregate increase of products within six years of $352,211,787; 36 per cent. against an increase of population of 17 per cent.

During this period the South has advanced in wealth $933,104,097, or 42 per cent. In 1880 the assessed value of property per capita was $160.60; in 1887, $193.35; increase $32.75.

Alabama has increased threefold in its manufactories since 1880; Georgia has nearly doubled. Kentucky added 30 millions to her manufacturing capital; Tennessee 28 millions; North and South Carolina about 17 millions each. There were 34,563 factories in the South in 1880 and 1887 showed 54,176 with an increased capital of $192,459,000 and 172,328 more hands employed in the latter than in the former year.

The building of railroads has been a great factor in Southern prosperity, ten years ago communication with the outside world was difficult and expensive; now they have extended their iron arms in all directions, giving access to a ready market of the products of millions of acres of land which had heretofore been worthless, and converting into countless wealth those vast forest of timber which have been undisturbed for so many centuries.

NORTH & SOUTH CAROLINA.

HISTORICAL AND GEOGRAPHICAL.

The Carolinas were explored by the French in 1563 and named in honor of Charles IX, (Carolus) King of France. Sir Walter Raleigh received a patent in 1584, and made the first English settlement in the United States, the colony soon afterward abandoning the State. A second futile attempt was made in 1587, and a few years later Raleigh was beheaded by order of James I, on a charge of treason. About 1640, and afterwards, the county of Albemarle, N. C., was settled by refugees from religious persecution, who had left New England and Virginia. In 1663 Charles II, King of England, made various grants and the old French name was continued in honor of the second Charles. But for further details we must refer the reader to history and pass on to present issues.

The Carolinas, claiming their original sovereignty, entered at the head of the Southern States in the recent armed protest against the predominance and sectional legislation of the Northeast. The fortunes of war decided against them, and they have accepted the result in good faith. No States in the Union are more faithful or truer to their pledges. The system of slavery (originally forced upon them and repugnant to the moral and religious sentiment of the world,) has been abolished and these States are now on the highway to manufacturing and industrial success.

The Carolinas lie principally between $32°$ and $36\frac{1}{3}°$ north latitude. The coast lands are interspersed with numerous bays, sounds and inlets, and are too flat to be attractive or healthy.

The low country of the eastern portion of these States are covered with a small growth of pine, and the middle country is comprised principally of the low sand hills which have a clay subsoil and give good rewards to the husbandman. West of this is a belt called the ridge, where the land rises abruptly and continues to ascend, exhibiting beautiful alternations of hill and dale, till it terminates at the extreme northwest in the Blue Ridge, the highest peak of which is Mt. Mitchell in North Carolina that has a greater elevation than any other point east of the Rockies.

MINERALS, PRODUCTS, ETCETERA.

The granite and limestone formations are numerous and beautiful. Copper, iron, lead and bismuth are found in the various sections and the richest deposit of bone phosphate on the continent comes to the surface in Charleston county, S. C.

South Carolina has its sulphur and magnesia waters at Glenn Spring, in Spartanburg County, and its picturesque cascades at the Falls of Saluda, in the mountain country, where the waters have a descent of from 300 to 400 feet, and North Carolina has within her borders the most famous mountains of the Blue Ridge and a great diversity of scenery and climate.

The products of the State are diversified, the low land being adapted to rice, corn, cotton; the oak and pine lands of the interior to cotton, corn, potatoes, tobacco, etc., and the pine uplands to fruits and vegetables. Bordering on the mountain range of the Blue Ridge, wheat, barley, corn and oats flourish, while apples, peaches, pears, plums, grapes, and small fruits in general grow luxuriantly. The fig tree thrives up to an elevation of about 1,000 feet. The principal soil of the State, excepting on the coast, is a red clay with slight admixture of sandy loam.

HEALTHFULNESS AND SALUBRITY.

Statistics show three-fourths of the days as clear and pleasant while the climate in general is very equable and excelled in this respect by few States in the Union. The central and high lands of the State are timbered with walnut, pine, elm, oak and hickory. The average daily range of temperature on the coast is a fraction less than at Santa Barbara, Cal., the heat of summer seldom exceeding 95°, and but few weeks in winter remaining at the freezing point. In point of healthfulness, picturesque scenery, and prospects for future developments the Piedmont region of this State is very desirable. Salem is located in one of the healthiest sections of the United States and is fast gaining a reputation as a favorable resort for invalids.

This section of the State is eminently salubrious, presenting as it does a favorable exhibit of all the features essential to health, such as elevation, drainage, dryness of air and exemption from epidemic and malarial visitations. Situated so high on sandy and porous soil, which drinks in the rain and prevents humidity of atmosphere and the noxious influences consequent upon the decomposition of vegetable and animal matter and removed far from the miasmic generation of stagnant marshes and ponds, this place is comparatively free from zymotic diseases, and absolutely so from those of a malignant or epidemic character. Innumerable witnesses testify to the advantages to be derived from a residence here in the treatment of that class of diseases which depend for their cure upon climatic influences, such as pulmonary affections, (including consumption, bronchitis, and asthma), or upon a change of climate, as dyspepsia, liver and kidney diseases, and rheumatism. The city is among the healthiest of its size in the United States.

SOCIAL STATUS, DESCRIPTION, ETC.

The geographical situation of this place makes it one of the most pleasant localities in the State; the topographic conformation, equable and salubrious climate, clean, high and shaded streets, the ample, highly cultivated, and tastefully arranged grounds that surround its dwellings, conspire to attract to and make this one of the most desirable and inviting places of residence in the State; and the number who are allured here from year to year, to escape the rigors of a Northern winter are steadily increasing. In order to create a city, in the true meaning of the word, it is necessary that its inhabitants should regard it with pride and affection, and also as something of which they are a personal part. The nationality or nativity of no man is questioned here. Whether he comes from the North or the South, or the East or the West, he will be gladly received, if he only possesses and practices the virtues that are essential to good citizenship.

The Twin City with its coming railroads completed, will have grand distributing advantages, and should make a great wholesale centre. It will then be an active railroad centre, and no idle dream that she is, indeed, a progressive city. In nearly every article of this sketch, although may have a personal heading, will be found some interesting fact or conclusion to be drawn. We invite you to read the entire work, as some point of information obtained may be valuable to you at present or for future use. This city will bear the closest scrutiny, and in the name of its progressive citizens, we invite all to come and spend a week, investigate the merits of this favored section, and we are certain that before the blizzards of another winter arrive, you will have concluded to take up a permanent abode here.

Situated in the uplands of the State, with several railroads competing for its freights to the tobacco markets, manufacturing centres of the North, and ports of exports to all parts of the world, this place will have advantages unequalled by any interior city of the South for the handling of all staple products. These new railroads concentrating here will secure a low rate of freight to Norfolk, Baltimore, New York, Boston and Philadelphia. This competition secures that quick transit so essential in mercantile trade. In addition to this, our tobacco is very desirable from its fine color and flavor, unsurpassed for its chewing and smoking qualities and of excellent staple. These substantial reasons can scarcely fail to open up to the central and upper portions of our State a market which, for many reasons, it is largely for the interest of producers to patronize.

Thirty tobacco manufactories are already in operation here and the field is especially inviting to the production of cotton goods. A dozen mills of that description, with their contingent industries, would not be out of place. Extensive wood manufacturing, and many other fields of industry, might be profitably engaged in as the weather is equable the entire year, and but little expense required to keep away the chilling blizzards of the Northwest, which lose their power for harm while climbing the Blue Ridge Mountains.

Our article on agriculture and thoroughbred stock will convey a slight idea of what advantages the surrounding country is possessed. The importance of those pursuits will be manifest, as thriving agricultural and stock-raising districts give back-bone to commercial and manufacturing centres. Any man who has the stamina to go west with limited means, and trusts to his energy and the smiles of Providence, and who succeeds there, could take the same energy and trust and have greater certainty of success in the South. He has no grasshoppers, nor enduring ice, nor snow, nor blasting drought, nor violent winds. His wants are fewer and his hardships less.

MANUFACTURING AND INDUSTRIAL.

It is eminently proper in a descriptive review of this character that the men or corporations who have really *done something*, who have ventured their time and means to the establishment of industrial works, and liberally dispensed their money in our midst for the construction of buildings, salary to employees, and purchase of material, should have a deserving mention in these pages. Such instutions risk large sums of money in buildings and machinery, surrounded by inflammable materials, and it is but due that they should receive good percentages as a reward for their great risks, heavy outlay of capital and business tact required in their operation. As these industries use up the raw materials of the country at remunerative prices and dispense large amounts in weekly wages, which revert to the tills of our merchants and mechanics, the municipality can well afford to give them liberal inducements in the way of exemption from taxation or other subsidies. We reiterate what we have said before, that on thriving manufacturing industries the growth and continued prosperity of our city largely depends, and those who are working for its upbuilding should receive due credit.

It is despicable for any citizen to speak against his own city, and to say regarding any enterprise to further its advancement, "Oh, it's no use; you never can make anything out of this place." We are glad to note that there are very few here of this class, and those who feel so should move out and give place to others who are able to "see the day star of future greatness arising."

OUR ADVANTAGES.

In the pages of this pamphlet we shall give conclusive evidence as to the many advantages of Winston as a manufacturing, agricultural and commercial center and among some of the points of evidence which we shall present are the facts that we have a well-equipped railroad with two others projected, which we have good reason to believe will be completed within the next season, and which will greatly add to our advantages and facilities of transportation. Our city is in the midst of the tobacco, grain and iron producing district. Wheat, vegetables, poulty, fruits, etc., can be had at reasonable rates to feed the employees of the manufacturer, and for which the agriculturalist receives remunerative returns.

The supply of fuel is ample and cheap and there are but few days in the year that will not permit of free ventilation without inconvenience. The great manufactories of the North where for half of the year the operatives must be kept in rooms almost air tight and superheated to keep out the intense cold, thus depriving the system of the necessary oxygenation, cannot be otherwise than destructive to health, and it is little wonder that thousands die annually of lung troubles, nervous diseases or other similar prostrations, when we consider the immense strain upon the system while living in rooms in which the principal part of the oxygen is used to keep up the combustion of fuel, and the great contrast in going from these rooms to the outside atmosphere. These facts and many others of like import are fast sending the manufacturing capital of the North to the more saluburious and equable climate of the Southern States. Every manufacturer and laborer will readily see the advantages to accrue from a mild and salubrious climate.

We have one cotton mill in operation and others in contemplation which will probably be built during the coming year; three furniture factories, four large foundries and machine shops; two merchant tailoring clothing manufacturing establishments; one of the largest woolen factories in the South; saddle and harness factories'; three planing and wood working mills, besides numerous smaller industries, all of which are crowded with orders, and several projected enterprises which we have no doubt will soon become realities. There are two national banks here with a capital and surplus of nearly $400,000. But our greatest industrial work is in the manufacture of tobacco, the fame of which Winston has gained as a wholesale leaf mart and the high reputation of its tobaccos, extend far and wide.

Twin City has the best graded schools in the state, and fine private schools; 12 churches, a seminary of note, an opera house, electric light, water works, gas, street cars, projected, macadamized streets, and paved sidewalks. The mortuary statistics show a health record unsurpassed by any city of its size in the country. The elevation of the place is about 1,000 feet above the sea. Consumption seldom, if ever, originates in this section.

We do not expect this pamphlet to be a complete index, as from our inability to find the proprietors or other responsible persons, from whom to secure facts and dates, we shall sometimes unwillingly omit an important business. We do not claim perfection nor expect a book containing so much matter as the present issue, to appear free from errors, but we will endeavor to make a creditable sketch, one which we think will be generally accepted with satisfaction by our citizens and mailed to friends and customers throughout the country, or preserved for future reference. From a proper estimate we find that more than 500,000 separate and distinct pieces of metal will be required in the edition, and should our readers find a letter upside down, or other typographical or historical errors, we trust that they will kindly make their criticisms light.

The business men who subscribe for a number of extra copies should not lay them under the counter, as is sometimes done, and forget to give them proper distribution. This book contains many valuable facts and dates, and some person will while away several hours with pleasure and profit in perusing the same. It is due to your own interest and those of your neighbors who are interested with you, as well as to the upbuilding of your city, that you distribute all numbers placed in your hands during the next month or so. Mail them to your friends or turn turn them over to the Chamber of Commerce for distribution.

The greatest known depth of the ocean is $5\frac{1}{4}$ miles (25,720 ft. or 4,620 fathoms) not quite the height of the highest known mountain, Mt. Everest. The average depth between 60° north and 60° south is nearly 3 miles.

St. Peter's Church, will accommodate 54,000; Duoma, Milan, 37,000; St. Paul's in Rome, 25,000; St. Sophia, Constantinople, 23,000; Notre Dame de Paris, 21,000; the Dome of Florence, 20,000; the Cathedral of Pisa, 13,000; St. Marc. in Venice, 7,000.

"The permanent constitution of the Confederate States of America" was adopted at Montgomery, Ala., March 11, 1861, was ratified by Alabama, March 13; Georgia, March 16; Louisiana, March 21; Texas, March 25; Mississippi, March 30; South Carolina, April 5, 1861. These so called ratifications were submitted to the people.

SETTLEMENT OF SALEM.

MORAVIAN HISTORY.

While it is not our purpose to go into a detail of past history, it is only proper that we should make a brief reference to the people who settled this town and county more than a century ago. Bohemia and Moravia were first to protest against what they believed to be the unrighteous claims of the Romish Church and the Reformation became prominent under John Huss, who suffered martyrdom in 1415. From his memory arose that religious body officially named the *Unitas Fratrum* or Brethren's Unity, and more generally known as the Moravians. To be freed from the spirit of oppression many of the brethren fled to Saxony.

In 1557 a parish was established in Poland, but an anti-reformation was fostered by Ferdinand II in 1620–27 which crushed out this church leaving only a handful of the Brotherhood from whom the line of descent was continued. The foundation for the town of Herrnhut was laid in June, 1722, on lands donated to the Brotherhood by Count Zinzendorf, of Saxony, and this soon became their general rallying place. A large number of Moravians subsequently emigrated to Pennsylvania and from there, in 1752, Bishop Spangenberg, accompanied by five brethren, set out to select a location in North Carolina. Together with Mr. Churton, the surveyor and agent for Lord Granville, they traversed the wild forests of this section and after numerous hardships and privations selected the "Wachovia tract" which, with subsequent surveys, was made to contain 98,985 acres and covers what is now about two-fifths of Forsyth county. This was deeded to the society August 7th, 1753, and the first settlement was made at Bethabara, (now Old Town), a few months later. Salem was selected as the central town for the Moravian Brethren in 1765 and the first house was occupied the next year.

In 1857 a separation of civil and religious government took place, since which time Salem has held regular municipal elections.

The present generation might derive an instructive moral lesson by contrasting the privileges and discomforts which beset the first settlers, with the happy circumstances by which they are surrounded; such a contrast should inspire the latter with feelings of gratitude for the blessings which they now enjoy.

In reviewing the hardships and privations that these early pioneers must have endured to withstand the savage beasts and savage men, and lay the foundations of civilization with all its incumbent blessings, a feeling of reverence comes over us and we can only recall the memory of those hardy veterans and gaze upon the work they have accomplished with the most profound respect. We find much embraced in their personal history that would interest the general reader if space would permit, but the bounds of this article and the important pressing present, forbids our enlarging on those early scenes.

The industrious habits of the early settlers laid a good foundation for manufacturing and it is not surprising that with the advent of the railroad, industrial establishments sprung up on all sides and the growth of Salem's young offspring—Winston—has been marvelous.

The Wachovia Society believed in making the children learn useful trades and it is worthy of note that the first substantial house built in Salem,—1766—is still in use as a pottery and has some of the quaint old moulds dating back to 1774. The Salem water works built in 1778 were in use up to ten years ago when the demand for a larger supply brought the present system. It is said that the water works were much admired by President Washington on his visit to this place in 1791. There are very many interesting reminiscences of the past, some of the most prominent of which will be incorporated in subsequent articles, but as indicated on our introductory page, *the present* is our special theme and we pass to a consideration of

WINSTON-SALEM.

In 1848 Forsyth county was formed and a year later fifty-one acres of the Wachovia tract adjoining Salem was sold, for the new court-house and village site, at $5.00 per acre. This was platted and named Winston, in honor of Col. Joseph Winston, who represented this section of North Carolina in the Patriots' meeting of colonial days.

Winston is superbly located for a manufacturing center as the entire county is well watered, contains broad fields of meadow and bottom lands, and many streams of good water power.

Fifteen years ago the surburb of Winston (adjoining Salem, but with business center a third of a mile from its boundary), had less than 500 inhabitants. About that time she began a rapid growth and to-day her population is over 8,000. Every block is filled to the mother town, so that only a street divides the two, and as both live together in unity, they should be considered as one. The Twin-City has been accepted as the proper cognomen, although each place still retains its postoffice and separate municipal government. The old town now has a population of about 3,000 inhabitants, and the combined population of the two cities is estimated at 11,000.

THE TWIN-CITY.

Excepting in locating a specific business or street in all our writings, when we say this city or this place, we mean both Winston and Salem, as they are practically one, and inseparable in all their movements of progression, social position, &c.

There are immediate prospects of two new railroads, the exact developments of which we shall give before closing these pages. These, with continued progress in manufactories, etc., give to this place an exceedingly bright outlook, and it is no stretch of imagination to suppose that we shall have a population of 25,000 within less than ten years from the present date. Taxes are low, real estate has not reached a speculative boom and the large amount already invested in factories and machinery will ever be a prevention from a retrograde movement. With the best graded schools in the state, and the oldest and best Female Seminary in the South, together with several private schools and excellent religious advantages, the high social and moral standing of the Twin-City will always be a laurel in its crown of progress. The business men here are wide awake and pushing. While ready to welcome Northern capital and immigration, they are not Micawber-like, waiting for something to turn up, but are progressive. But few cities of this size can boast of as many men who are rated in the hundreds of thousands, and the number of brick residences or costly frame mansions clearly demonstrates that we have a large per centage of well-to-do citizens in this handsome and healthful city.

Winston had about 400 inhabitants in 1872, but the N. W. N. C. R. R., now a part of the Richmond & Danville system, reached here that year, and the first tobacco warehouse was opened by Maj. T. J. Brown. This caused a new era in the developments of this section. Although tobacco had been grown for a dozen years with good success there was no immediate outlet for the product and but little manufacturing was done.

MANUFACTURING DEVELOPMENTS.

In 1875, Winston had about 1,500 inhabitants and property valued at

$300,000, with five tobacco factories having an aggregate capital of less than $100,000. In 1880 there were eleven factories with an invested capital of $417,500, and giving an annual product of $750,000. The present status shows over thirty factories and invested capital of $2,000,000. The annual product is above $4,000,000. This is a great tobacco market and several hundreds of wagons come weekly, sometimes daily, from the mountains and surrounding districts, making the annual transactions in leaf tobacco foot up to about $1,500,000. Other manufactories here do an annual business of about $1,500,000 and the wholesale and retail transactions of the general merchants foot up to nearly $2,000,000 annually. In subsequent pages we shall go somewhat into detail in order to verify these figures and give the names of those who are prominent in manufacturing and mercantile pursuits.

FORSYTH COUNTY.

This county was formerly included in Rowan, and was formed from Stokes county in 1848. It was named for Col. Benj. Forsyth, a soldier of the war of 1812 to 1815, who was killed in a Canadian skirmish. It is situated in the north-western part of the state, with the Yadkin river as its western boundry. It is eminently fitted for tobacco raising. The yield on new lands ranges 500 to 650 lbs. and on old lands, with fertilizer, a much larger crop is often realized. The annual yield for Forsyth county is now over 4,000,000 pounds. The soil, climate and situation of this county, are peculiarly adapted to the growth of the vine, which yields in the most luxuriant manner, wherever the least attention is paid to it. As early as 1761 this record appears in the archives of the church in Salem: "Great abundance of wild grapes, nineteen hogsheads of wine were made in the three settlements." The Concord, Clinton and kindred varieties are the most popular, because they grow with the least attention. Others can be grown with ease. Sorghum grows finely, and is manufactured into syrups of a bright color, and pleasant taste. Broom corn of long staple and excellent quality, is raised on many of the bottom lands.

This county is hilly and undulating, well watered and adapted to the production of the most nutritious grasses. The orchard grass, blue grass, mountain grass and clover make excellent pasture and timothy makes good crops of hay, millet does well, milo-maize and other forage and food can be produced to perfection so that sheep and cattle can be raised easily, wintered cheaply and there is no reason why the production of thoroughbred stock and dairy cattle is not eminently practicable. With abundance of milk cows, on these fine grasses, could be produced first-class butter, and cheese manufacturing is not only feasible but the field is especially inviting to those skilled in its production. Even the poorer grade of lands in this section grows grapes to perfection and is adapted to peaches, apples, pears, plums, cherries, gooseberries, currants and small berries.

More than a hundred different varieties of trees are found in this and surrounding counties. Mica, iron, manganese, asbestus, and traces of gold are here; marble, granite, soapstone and sandstone are abundant, and the entire county is fairly settled up with an industrious, and peace loving community. However there, is room for a population three or four times as great. Lands are cheap and good citizens from any section of the country will be welcomed. An admirable feature of the agricultural lands of this section, is the susceptibility of the clay subsoil for retention of fertilizers to a degree unsurpassed by any kind of soil. Tracts that are much worn are thus easily revived and made to produce good crops. The county has over 50 grist and saw mills, twelve wagon shops, eight tanneries, four potteries and a number of tobacco and other minor factories outside of the Twin-City. There are ten villages, among the largest of which is Kernersville, eight miles east of this place on the N. W. N. C. R. R., and which town has about 1,000 inhabitants.

STOKES COUNTY, ETC.

Our mother county—Stokes—was formed from Surry in 1787, and named after a revolutionary colonel. It lies north of Forsyth and has an area of 440 square miles. It is generally quite level but becomes broken around the Sauratown mountains, which cross the county diagonally and form a picturesque scene, in plain view from Winston. Moore's Knob is 2,583 feet in height and was used by the signal corps of the United States Coast Survey in 1875-7. Dan River, the longest in the State, flows centrally through Stokes and with its net work of tributary streams gives excellent water privileges. It produces a fine grade of tobacco and about thirty factories are in the county.

Stokes county is adapted to all kinds of products raised in this county, and in some respects has even better agricultural advantages. It has several valuable iron mines some of which have been worked in a limited way for seventy years. Recently the Pepper Iron Mines have been purchased by Ohio capitalists at $100,000 and smelting furnaces will doubtless be established in the vicinity of Danbury. The ores found here are the red and brown haematite and the magnesite. They are admirably adapted for making a fine grade of iron and steel. Developments in mining and manufacturing are much needed in this section. There are outcrops of semi-bituminous coal in the county and feldspathic clay for fire bricks is found near Danbury, and soapstone. Mica mines have been worked four miles from Danbury. Limestone and marble are found in the county and the great need of this country is railroad transportation facilities. Danbury, the county seat is a thriving town, and there are several other good villages in Stokes county.

Surry, Yadkin, Davie, Davidson and contiguous counties are similar to Forsyth and Stokes in location products, etc. What all this section needs most for a rapid development is

RAILROADS.

This vast region through to and around Cumberland Gap, with its acknowledged mineral wealth and many fertile valleys, might well be termed, the railroad desert of America, for there is no other section that has been known to the white man so long and with so many valuable features of commendation that is still lying undeveloped. No thoughtful man can examine this region of hundreds of acres of unmined coal, with its mountains of iron ore, abundance of fire clay, etcetera, without expressing the greatest of surprise that it has not come to the knowledge of capitalists long before this and been a manufacturing district, with its thousands of blast and coke furnaces, rolling mills, cotton manufactories, and a million of attendant inhabitants.

Throughout all this vast country are immense forests which have scarcely known the woodman's axe and the great desirability of making a permanent outlet to its natural wealth cannot well be overestimated. From Winston to Cranberry is about one hundred miles, and a road could there connect with those now building to the Gap, where they will tap the air line across Kentucky. This connection would place Winston within less than 500 miles of Cincinnati with her twenty-eight lines of railroad, radiating to every point of the compass. It is strange indeed if a corporation cannot be formed to take hold of these advantages.

FEMALE ACADEMY.

SALEM, N. C.

An educational institution that has been successfully conducted for 84 years should be a just pride to the city in which it is located, and revered by its numerous and widely scattered *alumnae*. The Salem Female Academy was opened as a boarding school in 1804, having ever since continued its educational work without interruption. During this time more than 6,000 of its *alumnae* have gone forth to do their allotted part in life's field. The children and grand-children of its early pupils have in many instances been educated here, giving this academy a wide spread influence and well earned reputation. It is unsectarian in its teachings, but is conducted under the auspices of the Moravian church and strict regard is taken for the moral and religious welfare of the students. Pupils are associated together in room companies under the charge of the teachers, their habits carefully noted and every safeguard thrown around them. Beautiful grounds adjoin the buildings, of which there are several not represented in the accompanying cut. The sanitary surroundings are in excellent condition and judicious calisthenic exercises have been instituted for pleasure and physical development. The course of study is thorough, distinctive in its feature of individuality and covers every desirable field, but our space will not permit of an extended review of the curriculum, terms, etc., which can be secured on application to the Principal. The buildings are located in a pleasant and retired part of the quiet Moravian settlement of Salem, and the extensive private grounds are a delightful place for out of door recreation, surrounded by the beauties of nature.

Rev. J. H. Clewell, is Principal, and superintendent of the commercial course. He was educated at Bethlehem, Pa., and Union Theological Seminary in New York City. Rev. Edward Rondthaler, D. D., pastor of the Moravian church, and recent principal, is superintendent of the department of languages. Prof. L. B. Wurreschke, a graduate of a German University in Silesia, has charge of the Physical Science Department, and the chief position on the musical staff is now held by Prof. Geo. F. Markgraff, who, in addition to his training in the best Moravian schools on the Continent, has taken a course in the Berlin Conservatory of Music.

Every department has a full corps of instructors—in all, twenty-five teachers—each enthusiastic to accomplish the best results in education. The average attendance is about 220.

A Male Academy, or boys' preparatory school is run in connection with the Moravian interests here, in charge of a principal and four teachers, having an average enrollment of 150.

The Salem public school is in charge of Mr. Samuel Hege and a female assistant. Salem also has a colored public school.

PUBLIC SCHOOLS

OF NORTH CAROLINA.

It is well that our legislators have provided for the education of the masses, as from reason and intelligence must come our progress in civilization. North Carolina has more than a half million of school children, and of these, according to the latest returns, 353,481 were white. The per centage of enrollment and attendance at the public schools indicate that the opportunities have been accepted by the white and negro race almost in exact accordance with their respective population and a fair share of all who would naturally be expected to attend school have accepted the benefits to be derived from the public schools. Indeed the attendance is quite as good proportionally as in the New England and Middle States, but for want of sufficient funds, the school year in North Carolina is only a little more than one-third as long as in some of the Northern States. This is partly atoned for by the greater number of private schools in the South, but our public school system should be earnestly fostered as it must be our great reliance for the education of the masses. North Carolina's total population is 1,525,341, and assessed valuation $202,752,622, while her average annual appropriation for public schools is $671,116. The Southern States spend about twenty millions annually for schools and the entire United States $111,304,927.

THE COUNTY SCHOOLS.

Outside of the Twin-City there are about seventy-five schools in this county, with an average enrollment over 40, making an aggregate of 3,033 scholars. These are cared for by efficient teachers and under the general direction of Prof. A. I. Butner, a native of this county, who was educated at the Moravian schools and who has been for fifteen years past, principal of the Academy at Bethania. Supt. Butner reports a deep interest in the work and an upward movement in the county schools.

WINSTON GRADED SCHOOLS.

The first decided movement for the organization of graded schools in Winston was made in January, 1875 by Col. J. W. Alspaugh, Joseph Masten, deceased, P. A. Wilson, G. W. Hinshaw, C. B. Watson and others. A subscription was started and the

Legislature asked to appropriate the public money to the graded system. The people at first voted down the direct tax, but subsequently the system was adopted and active work begun.

If there is any one thing more than another of which Winston should feel a just pride, it is the excellency to which her graded schools have attained. Beginning in chaos, five years since, Superintendent Tomlinson, by the aid of well selected assistants and backed by a school board of superior intelligence, has wrought wonders and given to the Twin-City a justly earned reputation of having the best graded schools in North Carolina. The present school board are Col. A. B. Gorrell, chairman; Mr. W. A. Whitaker, secretary; R. D. Brown, M. W. Norfleet, and Col. J. W. Alspaugh. The building of which we present a cut on another page was planned by the Superintendent and cost $26,000. It is a two-story brick in T form, having a length of 190 feet and a depth, including Chapel or Assembly room of 170 feet. The imposing tower runs up four stories and with belfry and spire attains a height of 112 feet. It has nine recitation rooms, ample halls, a commodious library and office, all elegantly fitted up, and the library is worthy of special mention as it contains a most extensive outlay of pedagogic and other works which are a great auxiliary to both teacher and pupil, amounting in the aggregate to over $4,000 worth of books. Altogether both inside and out the building is handsomely designed and equipped and may well be termed the "Crowning Glory of Winston."

Julius L. Tomlinson is a native of High Point, a graduate of Trinity and later of Haverford, Pa. Subsequently he took a post graduate course and has now been for more than a dozen years engaged in school work. His efficient services here are too well known to need further comment.

Wm. A. Blair, 1st Assistant, is also from High Point, graduated from Haverford, Pa., in 1881, and from Harvard a year later, and then took a Ph. D. course at Johns Hopkins University. Prof. Blair displayed a marked ability as an educator and rapidly rose to prominence. He has been three years in the school work of Winston, is Superintendent of the State Normal School and editor of the *Schoolteacher*, of which we make note elsewhere. J. J. Blair, brother of the above and also a graduate of Haverford, Pa., is 2nd Assistant, and a very successful instructor. Mrs. S. G. Lanier and Misses Bettie Spicer, Nora Dodson, Pamela Bynum, Anna Barham and Annie Wiley, all efficient teachers have charge in their several departments.

Prof. Frank M. Martin, a graduate of Biddle University, of Charlotte, is principal of the colored schools and is assisted by two male and four female teachers, J. E. Foster, J. C. Albright, Mrs. C. B. Martin, Mrs. Bettie Cash, Misses Sallie Waugh and Emma McAdoo. The building for these schools is a frame structure in the eastern part of the city, which was completed last fall at a cost, including grounds and fixtures, of $8,500. The enrollment of the graded schools is nearly 1,100, about equally divided between the races.

MORAVIAN CHURCH.
THE BRETHREN'S UNITY.

In connection with the settlement of Salem we have given some Moravian history as the church had control of the land matters here for a hundred years after the purchase of the Wachovia tract.

The first settlers of Salem arrived in January and February, 1766. They were George Holder, Jacob Steiner, Michael Zeigler, Melchoir Rasp, of Pennsylvania, and Gottfried Praezel, Niels Peterson, Jens Smith and John Birkhead, from Europe. These were reinforced by additional emigrants from Pennsylvania in the coming fall, accompanied by Rev. Richard Utley, who became the minister of the parish. A two story church building was erected in 1766 which served a half dozen years as a house of worship when a more substantial church took its place. In 1772 a bell, weighing 2,758 pounds was brought overland from Pennsylvania, and which served as a town clock by tolling the hours. A two stop organ was also made that year and took the place of the trombones which had been brought from Europe with the first settlement of the place. The 1772 structure served as a "meeting house", until the present remarkable edifice was completed in 1800. A large pipe organ was built in the new church in 1799, which is still in acceptable use there. The church structure is an imposing brick edifice which would probably cost $20,000 to duplicate at the present time. It was erected by the individual labors of the brethren and a large donation from Brother Frederick Marshall, the leader in the Moravian settlement, but no record was kept of the total expense. The superstructure is surmounted by a town clock which strikes not only the hours, but the quarters as well. It has a convenient seating capacity for 800 people, and will hold on pressure a thousand souls or more. It is heated by furnaces, has kitchen attachments, pastor's conference rooms a large Sunday School Chapel, and is a credit to the people who worship there. The simplicity, industry and moral integrity of the Moravian Brotherhood has been widely felt in its refining influence over this section of country. The Salem Female Academy was established by the Southern Synod of the Moravian Church in 1802. The organizations of this section are Salem and its four mission churches, Eden, Friedland, Friedburg,

Hope, Macedonia, New Philadelphia, Olivet, Old Town, Bethania, Mt. Bethel, Providence and Oak Grove, numbering over 1,600 communicants —of whom, about 600 are in Salem parish. For eleven years past the Salem Church has been under the spiritual charge of Edward Rondthaler, D. D., of Pennsylvania. After graduating at the Moravian Theological Seminary, at Bethlehem, Pa., Rev. Rondthaler was a student on the continent for some time. The degree of Doctor of Divinity was conferred upon him at Chapel Hill, in this State.

CENTENARY M. E. CHURCH.

The first Methodist organization in this vicinity was at Pleasant Grove 2½ miles west of Winston by Rev. John Alspaugh, about 1836. A few years later a church was built at Jerusalem a mile north of the city. In 1852 the place of worship was moved to the court house, a lot was purchased and soon afterwards a small brick church was erected on the site of the present edifice.

The Methodist Episcopal Church of Winston was continued under the administration of Rev. W. W. Albea in 1854, and the present elegant edifice was erected about four years since at a cost of $27,000. It is one of the most commodious houses of worship in this State and would grace a metropolitan city. The style of architecture is modern and the building will accommodate 1,500 persons, the seating capacity of the main auditorium reaching about 1,000 and the annex, which opens out direct to the pulpit with rolling doors, will seat 500 more. The membership numbers about 550, among whom are many of Winston's able and influential citizens. Outside of the main congregation there are three Sabbath Schools and mission stations connected with this church, under the charge of Rev. C. W. Robinson. Rev. W. C. Norman, the pastor, is a native of Davidson county, graduated from Trinity College and has been fifteen years in the ministry, coming from Raleigh, where he had remained four years, to Winston, December, 1887. On a succeeding page we hope to give an illustration of the above handsome structure.

THE PRESBYTERIAN CHURCH,

of this place, was organized in 1862 and now has 165 members. The building erected the year of organization is entirely inadequate to present convenience and $11,000 has been subscribed towards a new place of worship which has already been commenced. There is a handsome parsonage on the lot which with the grounds is valued at about $6,000. The church is well organized, having a full corps of mission and aid societies, Sunday School, etc. The Ladies' Aid Society has accumulated nearly $1,400 in three years past, with which to purchase an organ for the new church. Rev. E. P. Davis, pastor, is of Rutherford county, this State, and graduated from Davidson College, subsequently taking a course in the Theological Seminary of Columbia, S. C., and has been eleven years in the ministry, occupying but two charges before coming to Winston.

BAPTIST CHURCH.

The Baptist Society was organized in 1871 and the present building erected five years later at a cost of $4,000. Several hundred dollars of additional improvements have since been made and others are in contemplation. A couple of years since a mission chapel was built on Broad Street at a cost of $2,500 and flourishing Sabbath Schools are held in each house. The church membership is 235. Rev. H. A. Brown, born in Rockingham county, this State, has been pastor for eleven years past. He is a graduate from Wake Forest College and served for three years as pastor at Fayetteville, N. C., before coming to Winston, where his earnest labors have built up a large and influential church membership.

METHODIST PROTESTANT.

The Methodist Protestant church was organized in 1842 in what is now known as Liberty. In 1850 a frame building was erected on the site occupied by the present building, and the headquarters of the membership was moved. In 1876 a brick house was built at a cost of $3,500. At present there are 210 communicants. Rev. W. E. Swain was made pastor by the conference of December 1887. He is a native of Washington county, this state, and was educated at Yadkin College, N. C.

ST. PAUL'S EPISCOPAL.

The Episcopal organization was commenced in 1877, J. C. Buxton, of Winston, and Miss Laura Lemly, of Salem, being the only communicants at that time. Shortly afterwards the church was built at a cost of $3,000. The present membership is about fifty-five and the parish is in charge of Rev. H. O. Lacy, of Connecticut, a graduate of Columbia College, N. Y., and later from the Berkley Divinity Institute, of Middletown, Connecticut. Rev. Lacy has been in the ministry for five years past, coming to Winston two years ago.

The colored people have Moravian, A. M. E. Zion Methodist, Baptist and Presbyterian organizations, most of these having comfortable houses for worship, and a good membership.

LODGES, SOCIETIES, ETC.

Salem Lodge, No. 289, A. F. & A. M., meets at Hunter's Hall, 1st Thursday night. It was organized shortly after the war and has about 45 members. E. A. Ebert. W. M.; A. C. Meining, secretary.

Knights and Ladies of Honor, Salem and Winston lodge, No. 367, was organized October 27, 1880 and has a present membership of 36. Meets 1st and 3d Tuesdays, over Salem post-office. T. B. Douthit, protector; C. E. Crist, past protector; C. B. Pfohl, secretary.

Salem Lodge, No. 36, I. O. O. F., meets in Odd Fellow-Masonic Hall, Tuesday evenings. It was organized in 1852, burned out in 1880, now has about 60 members. J. C. Bessent, N. G.; T. E. Reynolds, V. G.; H. T. Foucht, Sec.

Salem Encampment, I. O. O. F. meets at above Hall, 1st and 3d Thursdays and numbers 31 members. W. H. Hall, C. P.; J. C. Bessent, Scribe.

Winston Lodge, 167, A. F. & A. M. meets 2d Mondays. It was established December 8th, 1854, with P. A. Wilson, Sr., W. M.; Peter Fetter, S. W.; Jno. W. Hunter, J. W. P. A. Wilson, Jr., is the present W. M.; H. W. Foltz, secretary, and the membership 93. Postmaster S. H. Smith is Deputy Grand Master of the State.

Winston Chapter, No. 24, R. A. M., holds convocations 1st and 3d Monday eves. It was organized in 1853. I. P. Gibson, H. P.; Wm. W. Stedman, King, and Dan F. Dalton, Scribe. D. P. Mast is the present H. P., and Wm. A. Blair, Secretary.

Piedmont Commandery, No. 6, K. T., holds regular conclaves on the 4th Monday. It was organized in 1884 and has about 21 uniformed Sir Knights. H. T. Bahnson, E. C.; N. S. Wilson, Recorder.

Knights of Honor, No. 1673, organized June 1879, and has a present membership of 55. It meets 2d and 4th Tuesday night in Johnson's Hall. T. B. Douthit, Dictator; H. T. Bahnson, Reporter.

Liberty Council, No. 3, Junior Order United American Workmen is a beneficial society and was organized October last. It has about 40 members, and meets at the Masonic Hall in Salem every Monday evening. J. P. Stanton, Coun., R. A. Hauser, V. C.; W. L. Morgan, Secretary.

Winston Assembly, No. 6485, Knights of Labor was organized December, 1886, and has 160 members although many of them are not in present standing. This society meets in the Gray Block, Friday evenings. J. J. Robertson, M. W.; L. N. Keith, Secretary.

A. L. Assembly, No. 6655, K. of L. (colored) organized May, 1886, has 30 members. Meets at Knights of Labor Hall in East Winston, Tuesday nights. A. Gates, M. W.; J. H. F. Dabney, Secretary.

Salem Orchestra consists of 14 performers of high merit and has recently had a thorough training under the directorship of Prof. Robt. L. Carmichael, who has gained a prominence in that line.

The Salem Cornet Band has 12 instruments and is under the leadership of C. M. Levister, billing clerk at the Salem depot. G. H. Rights, of the *Republican* office has served in the capacity of special instructor of this musical organization for some time past. The band was organized over 50 years ago and has since been in constant service.

The Salem Philharmonic Society is under the leadership of Prof. Geo. F. Markgraff, of the Academy, and this, with the orchestra, band, etc., has given to Salem a reputation for a high order of musical talent.

Twin-City Cornet Band was organized January, 1887, and has seventeen performers, a majority of whom are experienced musicians, under the leadership of Dr. J. A. Blum. D. T. Crouse, a musician of prominence, officiates as musical director, and his training ability has given to the organization a high order of merit. The band meets Friday nights at Winston Fire Company's headquarters for drill.

CLUB ROOMS.

The Club Rooms of Winston are an honor to the city and have none of the immoral tendency so often found in places by that name. Dr. R. F. Gray, Mr. W. A. Whitaker and others consulted upon the propriety of this matter and decided that properly conducted rooms providing for evening recreation would enhance the morals of the city and a definite plan was consumated.

The Twin-City Club was organized in February, 1885, with Mr. Whitaker as first president and Dr. Gray has officiated as one of the executive committee since its commencement. The favor bestowed upon this resort after more than three years of continuance, is evidence of the wisdom of the movement. The club has superb rooms in the 3d story of the Gray Block, brilliantly lighted by electricity and elegantly furnished. More than a hundred members of the city *elite* are on the rolls and the institution is governed by a high moral sentiment. A magnificent dance hall, admirably arranged reading room, card and billiard tables, lavatory, etc., are part of the institution, but no profanity, betting or drinking is allowed nor anything offensive to the liberal minded christian. J. C. Buxton is president and B. B. Owens secretary.

The German Club has adjoining rooms to the Twin-City Club, but is a separate organization. R. L. Crawford is president, and E. C. Strayhorn secretary. An entertainment for those who trip the light fantastic toe is given every two weeks and the rooms are arranged to open out with the Twin-City Club rooms when so desired. The German Club is governed under like stringent moral regulation and has about forty members.

The Twin-City Temperance Reform Club was organized November, 1886, as a missionary temperance work, without political affiliation, with a nominal admission, and small monthly dues. It has an interesting reading room, well furnished by friends of the enterprise and presents a strictly moral place for recreation. The organization is between 300 and 400 strong, having a branch at Union Grove in North Winston and is contemplating one at Waughtown. J. Q. A. Barham is president, and C. D. Hunt secretary. S. H. Smith was one of the prime movers and its first president.

The Forsyth Riflemen was first organized at Germanton, Stokes county, in 1812, by Col. Benj. Forsyth, re-organized in 1846 for duty in the Mexican war and again in 1861 by Col. Belo. The present organization was effected June 7th, 1884, as Company A, 3d Regiment, North Carolina State Guard. Captain, W. T. Gray; 1st Lieut, J. C. Bessent; 2d Lieut., F. T. White. There are forty-three active men, equipped, with regulation uniform.

The Land Office management, officially styled the Board of Provincial Elders of the Southern Province of the Moravian Church, is a corporate body that has charge of the real estate matter of the Wachovia tract. About 1,000 acres of this remains and for the most part is good tobacco lands, in price from $12.50 to $15 per acre. J. T. Lineback has charge of the office and is secretary and treasurer of the company, having been connected with the business since 1855. He is also Treasurer of the Salem Congregation, which has large real estate interests, and in that department is assisted by his brother, J. A. Lineback.

The Twin-City Hospital Association was organized June 28th, 1887, for the charitable object of establishing a hospital for Winston-Salem. A building was leased by the commissioners of the two places and through the exertions of the ladies, was furnished and opened December last.

Over 20 patients have been admitted and success has crowned the efforts of those willing workers for the good of humanity. The hospital is supported by the 10 cent month dues of the 180 members and generous contributions from others. Mrs. Jas. A. Gray was first president and Mrs. Gen. Boggs officiates in that capacity now. Mrs. W. A. Lemly, vice president, Mrs. J. W. Fries, secretary and Mrs. J. F. Shaffner, treasurer.

The Twin-City has the full complement of literary, missionary, ladies-aid and other societies usually found in a progressive and refined city.

PRESS, ETC.

The influence and progressiveness of a community may be largely estimated by the number and character of its public journals and the Twin-City gives a good showing in that respect.

Blum's printing-house was one of the first in the state having been started in 1827. Through its papers almanacs and other publications it has wielded a wide influence and to some of these we are indebted for valuable dates. The excellency of its present work shows it yet to be on the progressive plane.

The *People's Press*, published by L. V. & E. T. Blum, is now in its 36th volume and retains many of its early subscribers. The Blums have a book business in connection with their publishing house and various other interests in Salem. The *Weekly Gleaner* was the name of the first paper started in 1829—and next year changed to *Farmer's Reporter and Weekly Chronicle*. The *Carolina Gazette* was started in 1841 to be suspended two years later. The *Press* was established in 1851 and still continues.

The *Western Sentinel* was begun in 1856 by F. E. Boner and James Collins. J. W. Alspaugh subsequently became owner and was succeeded by G. M. Mathes, Edward A. Oldham, and the present publisher, Vernon W. Long. Mr. Long is a graduate of the State University, at Chapel Hill and has shown a marked ability with the scissors and quill. The *Sentinel* has an extensive circulation and in addition to its newspaper fittings has been recently put in good condition for job work and these pages are printed from its new self spacing type.

The *Union Republican* was established in 1872 by Walser & Walker, and was a few months later purchased by J. W. Goslen, a native of the county and a graduate of Trinity College. The *Republican* office is well fitted as a newspaper and job office and a credit to the Republicans of Western North Carolina. It has a large circulation clearly demonstrating the fact that there is no ostracism on account of political preferences in this section, but that both parties are represented by an intelligent and reading community.

The *Twin-City Daily* was started four years ago and has met the requirements of our people as an organ for current events. It was commenced by Domb & Whitehead, making several firm changes before it came into the hands of its present proprietor, Jas. O. Foy, who first engaged as a partner with P. A. Snider in the publication of the *Daily*, from whom he afterwards purchased his interest. The *Daily* has advocated every movement for the city's good.

The *Southern Guardsman*, a paper on military and musical matters was established in 1885 by Edward A. Oldham, at that time Adjutant 3d Regiment, North Carolina State Guard, was suspended for a time and revived again in May, 1888, by Will N. Coley, 1st Seargeant, Company A., 3d Regiment, North Carolina State Guard. The *Guardsman* is the official organ of the State militia.

The *Schoolteacher* is an educational journal now in its second volume, and ably edited by Prof. W. A. Blair, a prominent teacher in our graded schools. It is a model of neatness and a great auxiliary to the progressive teacher.

The *Academy* is in its tenth volume and is published in the interests of the Salem Female Academy. It is an index of personal happenings around the school, letters from the alumnæ, literary writings, etc. Miss Emma A. Lehman, the editress has a wide reputation for the high character of her scholarly articles.

JOB PRINTING OFFICES.

C. G. Lanier has at this writing, one of the most complete job printing outfits in Western North Carolina and employs several hands in turning out the various classes of commercial printing. Williamson & Morris began the book trade here in 1882, connecting therewith job printing which department has been added to from time to time to meet the requirements and three presses are now run by steam, with all the auxiliaries needed for rapid and first-class work. The book store comprises a large line of school and miscellaneous works, news stand, blank books, stationery and show case goods. The entire business is conducted in the Liberty Block and was purchased from W. B. Williamson by C. G. Lanier a few months since. Mr. Lanier is a native of Davie county and has been a resident of Winston for the past six years. The *Anchor*, edited by Mrs. Mary C. Woody, of Greensboro, is printed at this office, and the *Schoolteacher*, before mentioned.

Stewart's Job Office is a credit to the enterprise of its proprietors, who are natives of this county, and have spent several years in the larger cities perfecting themselves in the printing business. In 1885 they fitted up their present enterprise in the Gray block, for commercial, book and news work. These gentlemen have had a wide range of experience and orders for any class of printing entrusted to them will be executed in good style.

POST-OFFICES.

The postal statistics of any community is a very good index to the growth and prosperity of the place, and we are pleased to note that both Salem and Winston have had a steady growth in the volume of business done for several years past. The list of post masters in Salem is a long one and the connection of names has not been preserved. T. B. Douthit, the present incumbent is a native of Davidson county, and a resident of Salem for thirty years past. He was in mercantile trade prior to taking charge of the post-office in August, 1885. Mr. Douthit arranged a new office and has a very convenient system of box delivery. He has also placed a collection box on Main street, near the Winston city line for the convenience of Salem citizens. The office is third class with a salary of $1,200 and the business has increased 25 per cent in the past three years. W. C. Crist, a native of Salem has officiated as assistant since the advent of Mr. Douthit to the office.

WINSTON POST-OFFICE.

A post-office was established in Winston shortly after it was made the county seat. J. P. Vest still residing in the Twin-City was the first postmaster and was succeeded by Nathaniel Banner, H. K. Thomas, J. A. White, and Mode Faircloth. During war times the office was discontinued for a couple of years, after which W. W. Albea, W. A. Walker, and J. F. Helen had charge prior to the appointment of the present incumbent. Samuel H. Smith is a native of Wadesboro, N. C., and engaged in the drug trade here about a dozen years ago. He was chosen Mayor of Winston by the Commissioners, upon the resignation of J. C. Buxton, who had been elected to the Senate, and later elected by the people. In August, 1885, Mr. Smith resigned to take charge of the post-office. The office has steadily increased in receipts and salary and will next month be ranked as a second class with a salary of $2,000 and additional allowance for clerk hire, rents, etc. This is the distributing point for five star routes in addition to its double daily railway service. About 6,000 letters are handled daily and the aggregate mail matter per month reaches 14,250 pounds. The postal notes and money orders handled average 532 per month, aggregating a sum of $5,000. John R. Walker, a native Winstonian, has been four years in the office as assistant postmaster, and Wm. H. Hitt, of Danville, Va., has had a long experience at the delivery window.

ELECTRIC LIGHT AND MOTIVE POWER COMPANY.

Nearly every progressive city has an electric light company and Winston's efficient Electric Light and Motive Power Company was incorporated in August, 1887. A good brick building was erected on 5th street which together with the machinery and fittings, has made the plant cost nearly $25,000. The system used is the Brush Electric. The arc dynamo is of 45 light power and is taken to nearly its full capacity. This requires about 10 miles of wire and the incandescent system with 450 light dynamo has nearly 15 miles of wire in use. A Ball engine and Erie City Iron Works boiler, both of 80 horse power, and manufactured at Erie, Pa., are in place and are doing satisfactory work. J. W. McFarland, for several years connected with the Brush Company, at Cleveland, Ohio, is superintendent and electrician; D. P. Mast, secretary and treasurer; W. A. Whitaker, president. The system has proven popular in Winston and has been highly complimented on its successful working.

Salem Gas Works was erected in 1859 by F. & H. Fries is still owned by the firm and supplies a portion of Salem's public and private houses with the illuminating fluid.

FIRE DEPARTMENTS.

Both cities have a well organized and effective fire department, thoroughly manned and in good working order. The *Winston Fire Company, No. 1.* has about 25 well drilled men in charge of Capt. A. J. Gales. This company has a La France steamer, and 1000 ft of hose, purchased in 1882 at a cost of $3,800. W. F. Keith, engineer.

The Salem Rough and Ready has 40 men, a Button steamer bought two years ago at a cost of $3,000, and is promply on hand when an emergency requires. Jno. Schott is Captain; F. H. Vogler secretary, T. E. Davis, Engineer. There are two fire inspectors appointed for each ward and all flues and other fire traps are carefully looked into at stated intervals and to this fact Salem doubtless owes much of her special exemptions from disastrous fires. Salem has the oldest fire engine extant, which was manufactured in England, brought here in 1785. It was in use for many years.

Salem Water Works first started in 1778, was changed to present system in 1878. A brick reservoir holds 60,000 gallons and the iron tank, 450,000 both being supplied from two large wells from which the pumps, run by water power, convey the fluid to the reservoirs. F. H. Fries is president, L. N. Clinard, secretary and C. A. Fogle, superintendent. These works were planned, surveyed and their construction superintended by the private enterprise of the individual members, with the smallest amount of cash outlay and furnish an excellent supply of pure soft well water.

The *Winston Water Reservoir* is situated on the summit where it gives good pressure and holds 1,000,000 gallons. It is also supplied from wells and the pumps run by water power from the old Belo foundry plant. The Winston Water Company was organized in 1880, but labored under considerable difficulty in getting a sufficient amount of stock taken. The reservoir was completed in 1883, and over 4½ miles of mains have been laid. The wells hold a quarter million gallons and the water is superb in all respects. It is gaining in popular favor and will in time supplant the private wells which in the thickly settled part of the city soon become impure from surface drainage. The city has 43 fire hydrants. T. J. Wilson is president of the company and G. W. Hinshaw, Secretary Treasurer and Superintendent.

BANKING INTERESTS.

The banking interests of a community are of great importance to the general welfare, and the standing of the men at the head of these institutions is a matter which concerns every person in the city. We can confidently refer to the banking officers of this city *en masse* as a strictly reliable, conservative, and enterprising set of men. The banks here are backed by good capital, judiciously managed, and a suspicion of unsoundness in any respect has never rested upon them. This condition of matters adds largely to the general standing of the Twin-City but the banking capital is less than half a million and it might with propriety be increased to double that amount.

THE FIRST NATIONAL BANK

was organized March, 1876, with a capital of $50,000, which was shortly afterwards increased to $100,000. The bank has a present surplus and undivided profits of over $65,000, has regularly declared 10 per cent. dividends and stands solid in all respects.

J. A. Bitting, a native of Stokes county, was elected as President of the institution upon its opening and shortly afterwards removed to Winston where he has assisted in developing manufacturing and other progressive matters of the city. J. W. Alspaugh is a native of this place, was a practicing attorney and negotiated loans for the capitalists of this vicinity prior to commencing the banking business as cashier of the First National on its opening in 1876. Col. Alspaugh was mayor at different times, for several years editor and proprietor of the *Sentinel*, and has been more or less identified with every movement for the public good. C. Hamlen, noticed in tobacco manufacturing, is Vice-President. L. W. Pegram, of this county, has been Teller and Assistant Cashier for 10 years past. P. W. Crutchfield and James Martin officiate as book-keepers and Paul J. Bitting as Collector. The Directors are the President, Vice-President, Cashier, J. D. Watkins and T. J. Brown.

WACHOVIA NATIONAL BANK.

was established in June, 1879, by W. F. Bowman, Wm. A. Lemly, Jas. A. Gray, E. Belo, J. W. Hunter and others, with a capital of $100,000 which was increased to $150,000 about two months later. The surplus and undivided profits at the present time amount to about $100,000, and the annual dividends of 8 per cent per annum compare very favorably with the best monetary institutions of the land. Mr. Lemly, the president is a native of this county and has been in the banking business for twenty years. He was elected to the responsible position as cashier of the First National Bank of Salem, when but 19 years of age and after officiating there a dozen years was chosen as cashier of the Wachovia upon its opening and held that position until the death of Mr. Bowman when he was elected president and Jas. A. Gray succeeded as cashier. Mr. Gray was born in Randolph county, came to Winston in childhood and was in the mercantile trade here for several years. He commenced with the Wachovia Bank as Assistant Cashier when the corporation was formed and was promoted to his present position upon Mr. Lemly's election as president. The directors are the president and cashier, J. C. Buxton, Eugene E. Gray, W. A. Lash, N. D. Sullivan, and J. W. Hunter. E. S. Gray and G. H. Brooks are book keepers and Wiley G. Gibson, messenger. The bank is popular among our people and holds average deposits of a quarter million dollars, the transactions aggregating nearly twenty million dollars annually. The new rooms being fitted up on the corner of Main and Third streets opposite the court house square are in the center of trade and will have every requisite for convenience and safety.

FORSYTH 5c. SAVINGS BANK.

This organization was incorporated in February last and has recently commenced a banking business. It is established under the State laws, which provide for the welfare of the depositors by restricting the loans to first-class securities, inspection by the State Examiner, and other wholesome protection. The Forsyth Bank is officered by honorable and conservative gentlemen and will furnish a good place for the deposit of small savings, each time—depositor becoming practically one of the stockholders. Eugene A. Ebert, a Salem manufacturer is president; J. M. Rogers, B. J. Sheppard and Dr. H. T. Bahnson, vice presidents; E. A. Pfohl, treasurer and V. W. Long clerk of the board. The trustees are C. Hamlen, H. E. Fries, G. W. Hinshaw, S. E. Allen, C. A. Fogle, J. W. Hanes, W. W. Wood, R. J. Reynolds, C. A. Hege, V. O. Thompson, C. J. Watkins, R. D. Brown and A. J. Gales.

MANUFACTURING INTERESTS.

On pages 2, 3, 6, 7, and 11 we have given some valuable ideas and statistics, regarding our manufacturing, clearly demonstrating the superiority of the South for industrial developments and the importance which these institutions are to any progressive city. It is but proper that we should begin the special descriptions of that line in the Twin-City with the firm which commenced prominent manufacturing in Winston-Salem over 40 years ago and which continues under the original name given to it in 1846.

F. & H. FRIES,
COTTON AND WOOLEN FACTORIES,
Flouring Mills, Etc.

Francis Fries, deceased in 1863, began wool carding in 1840 and a year or two later added spining and hand looms for the manufacture of Salem Jeans, a product which soon received a wide notoriety. Henry W. Fries, a brother of the above, who still continues an interest in the enterprise, became a partner in 1846, making the firm style F. & H. Fries, which remains unchanged. In 1848 this firm built a cotton factory, principally as an adjunct to supply the woolen mills with warp. This was equipped with 528 spindles and consumed nearly 100,000 pounds of cotton for its second year. Improvements were added from year to year to both the woolen and cotton mills and the consumption of raw material at the commencement of the war was about 150,000 pounds of cotton and over 80,000 pounds of wool. A cotton factory had been built in 1837 by the Salem Manufacturing Company, which under reverses and bad management suspended operations about 1856. The building was afterwards fitted up as the Wachovia Flouring Mills and later purchased by the Frieses, who have it in successful operation. These mills have 6 brakes of rolls turning out 50 barrels of flour daily and a pair of burrs having capacity for half as much more. Two pairs of corn rocks grind about 200 bushels of that cereal daily and both a merchant and custom business is conducted. In good grain years a sufficiency of wheat and corn is raised in this vicinity to not only supply the local trade but to furnish large shipments for the distant markets. These mills are under the direct personal supervision of H. E. Fries.

THE ARISTA COTTON MILL

was erected by the firm in 1880 and is a decided achievement in modern manufacturing. This structure was erected on the most approved plans of the successful New England cotton mills at a cost for building and equipments of about $125,000. It is well lighted and perfectly adapted to the business throughout. The mill is furnished with 6,480 spindles, 180 looms and every requisite for turning out superior goods at a minimum price. A year ago the motive power was found to be insufficient for the most successful work and a 200 horse power Corliss engine, built at Chester, Pa., was placed in position. This massive motor weighs 26 tons but works as smoothly and steadily as a sewing machine. The fly wheel is 20 feet in diameter, the rim and arm weighing 25,000 lbs., and the shaft and hub adding 10,000 more. The face of the rim is 28 inches in width and turns the machinery by aid of a belt 130 feet in length and which weighs 650 pounds. E. S. Miller has been engineer for the firm for the past 15 years.

The Arista Mills last year used 1,888 bales of cotton aggregating 855,417 pounds which made 1,727,627 yards of goods, besides 166,447 pounds of yarn.

The woolen factory consumed in 1887, 174,843 pounds of wool and produced 375,255 yards of woolen goods. The reputation of these mills is very wide some of their products having been shipped to China and other foreign ports and at present their orders are far in advance of the working capacity. The Frieses are noted for their generous dispositions and liberal dealings with their employees and the public. They employ over 240 hands and disburse large sums in weekly wages and in general improvements to our corporation. Firms of this character are important factors in the prosperity and substantial growth of the city. The firm is composed of Henry W. Fries, one of the original partners, and John W., Francis H., and Henry E. Fries, sons of Francis Fries, deceased.

John W. Fries is also individually interested in tanning, conducting that business on an extended scale. This tannery dates back to the settlement of the town and at present furnishes an excellent grade of leather.

Iron Working Interests.

C. A. Hege & Co., Proprietors.

The men who by genius, personal energy and industry have widened the scope of manufacturing and by their work made the Twin-City known in distant markets are deserving of appropriate mention in these pages.

C. A. Hege the principal owner of the Salem Iron Works is a native of this vicinity and after completing the machinists trade in Bethlehem, Pa., located in Salem about 15 years ago and started iron work in a small shed. With a lathe turned by horse power, his genius was developed and additions were required from year to year until the present time three story structure was erected in 1882 at a cost for grounds, buildings and equipments of about $30,000. Prior to 1887 Mr. Hege's industry was principally on plows and small foundry work. In that year he took out patents on an "improved set" for circular saw mills, which invention proved to be so accurate, convenient and easily managed as to create an immediate demand for it among mill men. Five years later, for the accomodation of this rapidly increasing trade, the present structure was erected with 23,000 feet of floor area properly heated and lighted, and thoroughly equipped with modern labor saving machinery. Mr. Hege's inventive genius has perfected machinery of practical utility in every department of the shops so that his force of men can turn out double the work usually produced with the same number of hands. Conveniences for handling heavy articles, lifting cranes and general labor saving devices enable the Salem Iron Works to produce a large amount of machinery. The Hege mills are so popular in the South that in connection with partners in Florida, he has recently started a branch shop for the construction of the new patent, any kind of wood working machinery and railroad repair work at Apopka, a growing town at a railroad crossing in Orange county, Fla.

The Salem iron works have an extensive sale for their improved Hege saw mills in over twenty states; also in Canada, South America, the West Indies, Australia and Siam. They also build engines, wood planers, and a general line of wood working machinery, for all of which they have an extensive trade, both north and south.

VANCE'S IRON WORKS.
SALEM, N. C.
J. A. Vance, Proprietor.

J. A. Vance was born in this county, moved to Salem 16 years ago and for a long time was engaged at Fogle Brothers' mills. Five years ago Mr. Vance started his enterprise in the basement of the new planing mill where he had access to a convenient power and has added iron working machinery until he now has a first-class machine shop. His specialty is saw mills of which he has about 50 working in this State and has perfected an iron bed wood planer that has become a favorite among the wood working trade and Mr. Vance is scarcely able to keep up with his orders for this new machine. Plumbing and gas fitting in this and surrounding cities is a prominent feature of his trade in which he employs a number of men. L. O. Butner, of Salem, is manager of this department, and J. J. Robertson, also a Salemite, is foreman of the machine shops. Repair work of all descriptions has prompt attention and with three machine shops here, manufacturing interests can have new machinery made or repairs attended to as expeditiously as in any other city of this size in the States.

WINSTON IRON WORKS.
MAIN STREET, WINSTON.
Kester Brothers, Proprietors.

The Kester Brothers are natives of Winston and both practical mechanics. Dan'l E. having for some years officiated as foreman in the Salem Iron Works. Several months since they erected a 2 story brick building on Main street and with the beginning of the present year furnished it with modern planers, lathes, drills, etc., for effective iron manufacturing. added on a fine foundry room and are now fully equipped for good work. A 20 horse power Tanner & Delaney engine and boiler from Richmond, Va., are in place, a small engine for running the fan to the blast furnace. orders for work have come in rapidly and the new firm starts off under favorable auspices. The Kester Bros. are young men of industry and push and will doubtless succeed.

Wood Working Interests.

FOGLE BROTHERS.
SALEM, N. C.
Builders, Contractors and Wood Workers.

The Fogle's great-grand-father came to this county in 1755 and the name has ever been a familiar one here. Augustus Fogle, father of the above firm, was a carpenter and the sons have been brought up in woodworking. The firm was formed in 1871, as builders and manufacturers of sash, doors, &c. Additional buildings and machinery were added from year to year as their business required, and the present two story brick, of plain architecture, was erected in 1883. It is 60x120, fitted with the best of machinery and furnishes handsome and convenient rooms. The old building 30x120 and two stories is also occupied in the business. The Arista Mills and many of the best business buildings and private residences in the Twin-City have been built by the Fogle Brothers. Their dealings with customers are very liberal and a large number of laborers and mechanics have secured homes by having long time payments that could not have done so otherwise. All kinds of doors, sash and building material is turned out, requiring about 100 car loads of lumber annually in addition to that purchased in this section. Besides builders' material this firm manufactures 50,000 to 65,000 tobacco boxes annually; giving employment, in their different departments, to an average of 50 to 65 men and making this a business of no mean importance to the prosperity of Salem.

MILLER BROTHERS.
CHESTNUT AND 1ST STS., WINSTON.
Contractors, Sash, Door and Blind Manufacturers.

The firm of Miller Brothers, G. L. and J. S., commenced in 1872 as builders and five years later the mill was added. In 1884 J. S. retired leaving Gideon L. as sole proprietor. A few months later the mill was burned entailing a severe loss, but Mr. Miller soon afterwards erected the present fine two-story structure 55x120. The yard is on First street, running from Chestnut to Depot. Convenient engine, boiler and dry houses, all of brick are near the main buildings. The lumber yard is systematically arranged with incline tracks running into the mill. G. E. Miller accepted a partnership two or three years since and restored the old name of Miller Brothers. G. L. has been for over 20 years an active mechanic and fully understands every feature of the trade while G. E. has had 15 years of experience. The firm erected the Methodist church described elsewhere, the Farmers' Warehouse, Gray Block, J. A. Gray's fine residence and many of the principal business and private residences of the place. The location of the mill is in close proximity to the depot giving easy access for shipments. The buildings have first class equipments for sash, doors, blinds and other wood work and the lot 210x270 gives every needed facility for rapid and perfect work. An average of 40 men or more are employed and Miller Brothers deserve a full share of credit for the improvements and architectural beauty of the Twin-City.

N. C. FURNITURE COMPANY.
SALEM-WINSTON, N. C.
Wholesale and Retail Furniture.

The development and success which has attended wood manufacturing in North Carolina during the present decade is sufficient to warrant us in expecting more rapid growth in that direction than we have heretofore attained. R. Stevens of Pennsylvania opened up a retail furniture store in Winston a couple of years ago. Being a practical cabinet maker he concluded to manufacture goods for his custom, a year since formed an alliance with the proprietors of the Salem Iron Works and commenced the enterprise. It was at first only designed to supply the home demand, but the proprietors added the best of wood working machinery from month to month until they now have one of the best equipped furniture factories that is to be found in the South and are securing an extensive wholesale trade in the Carolinas and Virginias. The lumber is principally secured in this section of country and with the advent of railroads into the forests of Western North Carolina, walnut, poplar and oak will be cheaply and easily procured. The North Carolina Furniture Company have a retail store at the corner of Third and Liberty streets in Winston, under the management of J. C. Simmons and the manufactury is at the Salem Iron Works, where the advantage of saw mill, planers and special machinery perfected for this business gives them every facility for rapid and good work.

CICERO TISE.
MAIN STREET, WINSTON.
Furniture and Undertaking.

Cicero Tise is a native of Winston and was for a dozen years employed in the merchandising. In 1877 he commenced the furniture trade and has added to the business until he now has one of the most complete assortments in this section of country. Jacob Tise, father of the above, erected the handsome galvanized iron front building, on Main street, opposite the court house, in 1887. This structure is 40x100 feet, three stories and basement and its architectural beauty would grace a metropolitan city. Six months ago the basement was fitted up with machinery for producing the ordinary grades of furniture and several hands are now employed in that work by Mr. Tise, under the superintendency of H. D. Holcomb, of Pennsylvania. J. H. Pegram an experienced man,

has charge of the undertaking department and every requisite for burial service is furnished from this well known house. In addition to all kinds of furniture, from the common grades to expensive parlor suits, Mr. Tise also keeps a full line of house furnishing goods, carpets, wall paper, refrigerators, stoves, china vases, etc., and carries an assortment of buggies as well. A steam elevator runs from basement to garret and a finishing room 40x50 in an adjoining building opens into the second story.

A. C. VOGLER & SON.
SALEM, N. C.
Undertaking and Furniture.

A. C. Vogler is a Salemite, and after a five years apprenticeship with the venerable John D. Seiwers, he opened up a cabinet shop on his present site, thirty years ago. Mr. Vogler added ready made goods to meet modern progression, now has a good assortment of furniture, ordering the finer grades by sample, when desired. This house manufactures common coffins and furnishes fine caskets to meet his demand in undertaking. In this line his trade spreads out over a wide territory, and with a quarter of a century's experience, every requisite to the last sad rites is carefully looked after. With January '87, Mr. V. admitted his son Frank H. as a partner. Frank has since received a diploma from the Oriental School of Embalmers, and is secretary of the North Carolina Undertaker's Association. The trade of the firm extends out for a radius of twenty miles or more, and needs no further comment from us.

WINSTON AGRICULTURAL WKS.
DEPOT STREET.
Tate's Victor Grain Separator.

The Winston Agricultural Works was incorporated in 1884 for the manufacture of Tate's Victor grain and seed separator, a most useful invention for the farmer, as from its simplicity, it is eminently practicable. We hope to see the manufacture of this machine pushed to the extent of its merits.

Wagons, Carriages, etc.

GEO. E. NISSEN & CO.,
SALEM P. O.,
Waughtown Wagon Manufacturers.

John P. Nissen, father of George E. and Wm. M. Nissen, of the above firm, commenced the wagon trade two miles southeast from Salem P. O., in 1834, and up to the time of his death in 1874, had sent out more than 5,000 wagons. The business continued to increase, now averaging 500 to 700 wagons yearly, and making a total output up to the present time of over 11,000 wagons of the J. P. Nissen brand. The firm owns a mill at Panther creek, in Yadkin county, and purchase besides a large amount of lumber from the mills of this and surrounding counties. The factory comprises a number of buildings, the most conspicuous of which is the mill, whose tall smoke-stack is noticeable miles away. A 45 horse-power Westinghouse engine runs the machinery, which comprises spoke and hub lathes, circular saws, planes, shaping machines, tenoning devices, and other inventions suited to the business in hand. Another small engine supplies the blacksmith shop with power. This shop is a peculiar shaped building, presenting twelve sides and contains twelve forges. There are two wood working shops, two paint shops, besides minor buildings and sheds. The business gives employment to some fifty or sixty workmen—were it not for the labor-saving machinery employed this force would necessarily be very much greater. Material is kept on hand for three or four years supply, in order to have it thoroughly seasoned. The hardware stock is of superior quality, and the required sizes and lengths to work advantageously, is made by a Pittsburg iron firm. The copartners have grown up in the factory, and wagon making has been the business of their lives.

J. A. WHITE & SON,
LIBERTY STREET, WINSTON,
Tar Heel Cart, Carriages, & Buggies.

Jas. A. White began the carriage trade 25 years ago with J. T. Steiner in Salem, and in 1871 started business in Winston, later, accepting his son, Joseph O., as partner. All kinds of carriages, buggies and repair work is attended to, but the great specialty of the firm at present is their own device, patented January, 1887, and known as the "Tar Heel Road Cart." This vehicle is possessed of many features of merit, and is made with double or single seat at prices from $30 to $40. The firm have sold about 150 of these in this State alone and when rightly found out this patent should bring to J. A. White & Son a comfortable fortune. A factory for spoke, hub and bent works here and another well equipped for the manufacture of the "Tar Heel" alone, would pay well.

F. C. MEINUNG,
SALEM, N. C.,
Carriages, Buggies, Etc.

Henry E. Meinung, deceased, commenced the carriage business in Salem over half a century ago, and A. E. Giersh, who began blacksmithing for the shop in 1837, is still at the forge. The business was turned over to the son, F. C. Meinung, four years ago, and he continues the old hand-made goods at the sign of the "Red Wheel," in Salem, giving special attention to custom and repair work.

There are several wagon repair and blacksmith shops in the Twin-City, but our space is limited, and we must pass on to other matters.

You should preserve this pamphlet for future use.

Miscellaneous Industries.

SALEM HOSIERY MILLS.
ELM STREET, SALEM.
A. G. Hough & Co., Proprietors.

The Salem Hosiery Mill was started some four years ago and the firm has recently erected a two story brick structure on Elm Street. They have machinery for turning out about 50 dozens of seamless half hose and give employment to some 30 girls. The product although of excellent grade goods was at first hard to dispose of, but now finds a ready sale in the Northern markets at paying prices and has become one of the established industries of Salem. Mr. Hough is a native of Davidson county, having been variously engaged in farming, official positions, editorial work, etc. R. A. Spaugh, the other partner, was born in this vicinity and officiated as book-keeper in the Salem Iron Works for a long time.

SALEM PAPER MILLS.
SCRANTON & LEE, PROPRIETORS.
Manilla and Grey Wrapping Paper.

The Salem Paper Mill was first started in 1885 and came into the hands of its present proprietors about a year since. It is fitted up for the manufacture of wrapping papers, making from rags, about a ton each day of manilla, or grey shades and which is sold to North Carolina dealers. It is run by steam and gives employment to some ten hands. Both the partners are from New York state and Mr. C. F. Lee, the manager has been for 30 years in the paper manufacturing trade. The small manufactories all lend assistance to the cities' growth and we hope to see many more of them come.

SALEM BROOM FACTORY.
MAIN STREET, SALEM.
W. O. Senseman & Co., Proprietors.

The manufacture of brooms was begun here in a small way a couple of years ago, but the demand is extending, and the above firm have during the past month put out about 250 dozens of this indispensable household article. The firm ship their broom corn from Chicago, paying high freights, and as there is much land in this section thoroughly adapted to its growth, some of our farmers would consult their own interests by planting out a sufficient acreage to meet the home demand at least. The above firm will be glad to advise with those who contemplate growing the product.

I. W. DURHAM.
FOURTH ST.,
Marble and Granite Works.

I. W. Durham is a native of Charlotte and learned the marble cutter's trade there, coming here a dozen years ago and shortly afterwards commencing in the marble and granite trade. Mr. Durham handles all kinds of desirable, domestic and imported marbles and granites. Native granites of good consistency and taking a fine polish are found in abundance from four to twelve miles from this place, and Mr. Durham has superior facilities for meeting every demand of his trade.

J. A. Bennett, of Salem, also has a similar marble business on Main street, opposite Brown's warehouse.

SALEM BONE MILL
AND COTTON GIN.
Dr. J. F. Shaffner, Proprietor.

The acreage of cotton raised in this county is small, and the only cotton gin in Forsyth, owned by Dr. Shaffner, gins but little more than 100 bales per year. This was established in 1882, and the doctor has since added a bone mill, which makes a market for old bones, and on account of the scarcity of raw material, is limited to about 50 tons per year, of this valuable fertilizer. In 1884 Dr. S. built a tobacco factory in Salem, 55x80, three stories in height, which is now used as a leaf house by Edmunds & Gilmer.

THE TOBACCO INTERESTS.

On pages prior to this we have mentioned the tobacco interests of this locality, illustrating on page 6 the desirability of the Piedmont tobacco and on page 11 giving some aggregate statistics of the Twin-City manufactories. It now remains for us to write a more exhaustive sketch of "the weed" and under notice of the leading firms in that line to give additional facts, for to this industry, Winston especially owes a very large share of her development.

It has been demonstrated beyond a doubt that for chewing purposes no other section of country produces a more desirable color and flavor than the highlands of western North Carolina. Tracts that are comparatively poor, can be made to produce from 500 to 800 pounds per acre and although many other states raise double this amount, the grades are inferior and the net yield in dollars and cents is more here than in sections of country that grow a greater number of pounds to the acre. Tobacco for domestic use has been raised in this region for a half century, but a new impetus was given to the business about 20 years ago. Guthrie, Marshall and Kirby, experienced tobacco growers from Virginia had located in Forsyth county some years previous and by judicious tillage had fully demonstrated that western North Carolina could be made to produce as fine leaf for chewing tobacco as any section of the globe. There are but few states, if any, where the soil has been found to be as well adapted to the superior grades of yellow and mahogany leaf as this, so that we now practically have the monopoly and there is every reason why this industry should continue to develop. The fine textured tobacco will thrive up to an elevation of perhaps 4,000 feet above the sea, and way up on the cliffs of the Blue Ridge are found the hardy mountaineers who grow a small "crap of tobacker," which is indifferently cared for, dried in the sunshine, and what he has above his own needs is brought to market with which to purchase a few necessary articles of merchandise. The more thrifty farmer who plants out a fair acreage of the favorite kinds and looks after the proper cultivation, curing and marketing with care, often realizes from $200 to $300 per acre for his product and as these high lands can be purchased cheaply many northern emigrants will doubtless soon engage in this kind of agriculture.

From year to year the business has rapidly widened and now within a radius of 30 miles from this place, the annual yield aggregates 8,000,000 to 12,000,000 pounds. This is nearly all sold at Winston and many wagons come 60 miles or more with tobacco, while large quanties of yellow and mahogany leaf are shipped from other points and marketed here. The number of persons in the Twin-City engaged in all departments of the tobacco trade foots up over 1,000 and those dependent upon the workers for daily bread would aggregate as many more. Our readers can depend upon the figures which we give as being *approximately* correct, for we endeavor as far as possible to exclude all over drawn statements. As a market for leaf tobacco, Winston has rapidly risen to the front and the success of the manufacturers is largely dependent upon the fact that they have daily access to the warehouses that furnish the finest grades of leaf for chewing tobaccos, in the world. The vast importance to Winston-Salem of this industry cannot well be over estimated.

TOBACCO WAREHOUSES.

To any one visiting Winston for the first time, its tobacco warehouses become objects of decided interest. Especially is this the case if a big "break" is in progress. Then can be seen gathered together 20 to 30 or more keen-eyed, thoroughly educated buyers—men whose senses are so trained as to enable them to tell to the fraction of a cent what this, that or the other grade of leaf is worth to the manufacturer or shipper. From 5,000 to 15,000 feet of the warehouse floor is covered with piles of tobacco leaf, ranging from 25 pounds to 1,000 pounds or more; the stentorian voice of the auctioneer is heard, a score of farmers are waiting with keen suspense, all anxious to know what his particular heap will bring. A halt of 15 to 20 seconds is made at each lot while the buyers examine the grade of goods and in turn puts in his bids, the weed is "knocked down" and the surging crowd pass on to the next pile.

Winston has four tobacco warehouses and in order to avoid too much repetition, we will say that all of these have basements, furnish ample storage for tobacco, stalls for horses, office accommodations and camp rooms for farmers. The countryman who drives to Winston has only to bring his forage for horses and provide something for his own sustenance, when he can live quite independent of hotels or livery stables, as the warehouses furnish ample rooms for roughing it, or "camping" as it is called. The annual sales of the four Winston houses aggregate 11,000,000 to 14,000,000 pounds yearly or about $1,500,000 in cash transactions.

Prior to 1872 no effort had been made to systematize the marketing of tobacco, the curing and handling were indifferently done and growers placed little dependence on the article as a staple crop.

Maj. T. J. Brown, a native of Caswell county, residing in Davie for some time, became impressed with the needs of Western North Carolina for a tobacco market and after prospecting at Madison, about January, 1872, decided to try Winston. By his request, G. W. Hinshaw extemporized a warehouse from a stable on Liberty street, and Maj. Brown opened up public sales in February of that year. Col. J. W. Alspaugh, Wilson & Gorrell, Dr. Shaffner and others uniting with Maj. Brown in the ideas of progression, came to his assistance in the erection of the old Brown's warehouse on Church street, which was completed in 1872 and which the major subsequently purchased entire. This was the real opening movement of making Winston a great tobacco mart. The daily auction sales brought together the buyer and seller, created a regular law of supply and demand and made a staple product of "the weed."

BROWN'S WAREHOUSE.

Lash's warehouse was erected in 1873, and continued in use for several years. The Planters' (now Piedmont) the same year and others subsequently. Brown's old warehouse did good service for a dozen years, the transactions under its roof aggregating several millions of dollars.

W. B. Carter, of Rockingham county, accepted a partnership with Maj. Brown, about 14 years ago and in 1884 the firm built Brown's warehouse on Main street which is a model structure of its kind and deserving of more extended comment than our space will allow. The main building is 90x200 feet the salesroom covering 18,000 square feet, without post, pillar or other obstruction. The building with grounds is valued at $20,000 and the enterprise is in every way a credit to its proprietors and to the city which gave it birth. J. Q. A. Barham, an auctioneer of twenty years experience acts as salesman and has few superiors. P. A. Wilson, Jr., has officiated as bookkeeper for several years past.

THE FARMERS' WAREHOUSE.

Col. A. B. Gorrell was identified with the first decided tobacco movement in Winston, was for sometime book-keeper and later a partner with Maj. Brown. The Col. is a native of Greensboro but came to Winston at an early age, and was a merchant of this city for several years. He has served our people as mayor, alderman, school commissioner and been closely connected with many progressive movements. G. W. Hinshaw, (a public spirited Winstonian, who will have further mention in the mercantile department), and others joined Col. Gorrell in 1881 for the erection of the Farmers' warehouse, which is a handsome and commodious structure on Liberty street. The Colonel gives his strict personal attention to the business and the Farmers' warehouse has made a steady increase in sales from year to year, which is gratifying to its proprietor, and evidence of his good business tact. G. E. Webb, of Durham has officiated as auctioneer of this house for three years. N. S. Wilson, a Winstonian is the efficient book-keeper.

PIEDMONT WAREHOUSE.

This structure was erected in 1873 by a stock company and was originally known as the Planters'. It was leased in 1876 by M. W. Norfleet, large additions made and the name changed to the Piedmont. The present building is 60x190 with an L 40 x70. Mr. Norfleet is a native of Caswell county, was engaged in Merchandising in Winston for a year or two, prior to commencing the tobacco business as proprietor of Piedmont warehouse. The sales of the house have increased tenfold since Mr. Norfleet came to the business in 1876. H. J. Crute, auctioneer, is a Virginian and has been with the Piedmont for four years past. The entire force of employees are attentive to their respective duties giving general satisfaction to both buyer and seller.

THE ORINOCO

is a fine brick structure 90x200 at the corner of Main and Second sts. It was built by a stock company, opened November 19th, 1884 with 400 piles of tobacco on the floor and has ever since been in successful operation. The firm operating the Orinoco is Gilmer, Wilson, & Co. Of Capt. Gilmer we shall elsewhere write in connection with the only exclusive wholesale house in town. He is also a leaf dealer, (firm of Edmunds & Gilmer). His partner, Mr. E. H. Wilson, is a native of this county, and the management of the business of the warehouse largely falls to him. This position is characterized by a class of work that calls for administrative and executive ability. The firm have the services of C. S. Matlock, an efficient auctioneer, and J. B. Taylor, of Henry county, Va., as book-keeper, besides the full corps of expert assistants usually required in the business.

MANUFACTURED TOBACCO.

Some manufacturing was done in this vicinity prior to the advent of warehouses. Maj. Hamilton Scales having been first to start the business in Winston. J. A. Bitting was by far the largest buyer in the leaf market during 1872-3, shipping his purchases to Georgia for manufacture. From year to year our enterprising business men discovered that a good leaf market presented extra inducements for the manufacture of plug and twist, and to-day the Twin-City has a world-wide reputation from her success in this industry.

Our tobacconists as a rule are men of whom the Twin-City may well feel proud. Generally starting with small means they have by sagacity, industry, and perseverance hewn out their own success and become the architects of the competency with which they are surrounded. Their dealings with customers and employees have been characterized by liberality and for generous aid to public enterprises no class of our citizens can be so universally relied upon. Without their bountiful assistance it would scarcely have been possible for so large and complete an edition of this descriptive sketch to have been issued. Yet most of these liberal donors would have been satisfied, if the general good had been properly covered, that we pass them by without a special mention. We have however decided to make brief personal reference to each important establishment; but in order to not occupy too much space we will generalize our matter as far as practicable. The attentive reader by this time must understand that Winston and Salem lie side by side and Winston being the city of latest developments has the larger share of tobacco factories, because building sites were here found to be more accessible. There are over 30 firms engaged in the trade and two-thirds of these have fine large structures, four to five stories in height, fully equipped with modern machinery, steam and hydraulic attachments, elevators, and every requisite for successful manufacture. Nearly all of these establishments use principally the tobacco grown in this State. The trade of our manufacturers covers most of the South and is rapidly gaining a foot hold in Pennsylvania, Ohio and other northern states. The larger firms manufacture their own tobacco boxes and caddies amounting to several thousands each year.

The tobacco business here is conducted upon a systematic basis, under wise regulations, by a Board of Trade, which confines its deliberations entirely to tobacco matters. Col. A. B. Gorrell is president, Frank A. Coleman, secretary; M. A. Walker, treasurer, and the committe of arbitration is B. J. Sheppard, J. W. Hanes and W. W. Wood. T. Barber is supervisor of sales.

P. H. HANES & CO.
Winston's Largest Manufactory.

In commencing the tobacco interests there are so many fine buildings and real large firms in the Twin-City that it is difficult to know where to begin; but we believe that even the competitors of P. H. Hanes & Co., accede to the claims of this firm as having the largest tobacco manufactory here. H. Scales, T. L. Vaughn and one other firm, (since gone out of business) were operating tobacco here when the above firm started in 1873. Hanes & Co., suffered by fire the loss of their buildings and and equipments in 1877 and soon afterwards erected about half of their present factory. Later an L was attached and subsequently another wing. It is a four story structure, fronting 125 feet on Chestnut street and extending back 155 feet. In order to get an adequate conception of the different features of manufacture it is necessary to take a tour through one of these establishments when the work is in progress and several hundred busy hands making plug and twist from the tobacco leaves. We will here only say in brief however that the leaf purchased from the warehouse is recured, packed again in piles, sorted for the different grades, stemmed, sweetened with licorice and sugar, to meet the requirments of different tastes and brands, made into twists or plugs, pressed, (in tobacco parlance prized) boxed and shipped to the trade. This firm employs over 300 hands during the tobacco manufacturing season. Last year their purchases of leaf was more than 1,200,000 lbs., of sweeting fifty tons, and after the loss from stems and otherwise the manufactured product made a net figure of nearly a million pounds. The favorite brands of P. H. Hanes & Co., are the "Missing Link," "Man's Pride," and the "Greek Slave" although, as with all other factories here, a number of other popular brands are made besides the leaders. The Haneses are from Davie county and have a thorough training in the tobacco trade. The monthly pay roll foots up nearly $5,000 and this disbursement serves as a very important factor in the prosperity of our city.

BROWN & BROTHER.
Plug, Twist, Navy and Smoking.

One of our largest and most prominent tobacco manufacturing firms is that whose name heads this article. Dr. W. L. and R. D. Brown first began making tobacco at Mocksville, Davie county, over twenty years ago. Their factory was unpretentious, but it proved to be the opening wedge and prepared them to start aright in the business of Winston, which they did in 1876. They erected a structure 50x150 feet, four stories and have since added over 50 feet additional to the length, besides building an L 34x60 feet. Brown & Brother employ on an average 250 hands and make an annual output of nearly three fourths of a million pounds. During the busy season some $4,000 per month is disbursed for wages and the average paid for leaf tobacco is probably double this amount. The product of the factory is plug, twist and navy, medium to fine grades, and granulated smoking tobacco. Perhaps the most favored brand is the "Old Oaken Bucket," of which they are the sole proprietors, packing it in 25lb buckets. The "Waverly," "Stonewall," "Cottage Home," "Peace and Plenty," "Slap Jacks," "Little Neck," "Our Q," and others have a popular run. This firm buys large quantities of burley tobacco from the Louisville market which they work into "navy" for their general trade. Both of the partners give personal attention to the business and with efficient superintendants throughout, everything is done in order. T. A. Wilson has for eight years past officiated as bookkeeper.

R. J. REYNOLDS & CO.,
Plug, Twist and Fancy Tobaccos.

R. J. Reynolds is a native of Patrick county, Virginia and has been in a tobacco factory from boyhood. He commenced business in Winston in 1875 and has kept pace with the trade, increasing his facilities from time to time. His factory has a wing, three stories and basement, of 38x215 feet, and brick addition 50x50, making it front 90 feet on Chestnut street, the buildings, grounds and equipments being worth fully $25,000. The annual output of this factory is between one half and three quarters of a million pounds. Mr. Reynolds says that 1888 starts off with as bright prospects as any previous year and he expects the factory to eclipse the former record. Recently W. N. Reynolds, a younger brother and Henry Roan, an old employee of the office, have been admitted to an interest in the business and the firm style is now R. J. Reynolds & Co. From 250 to 300 hands are employed, thus giving disbursement to a princely sum of cash which speedily finds its way to the coffers of our merchants and mechanics. Some of the leading brands of this factory are the National, R. J. R. (trade mark), and World's Choice. Mr. Reynolds deals exclusively with jobbers and has no salesman on the road, the merit of goods being a sufficient advertisement to bring sale for all the manufacture of the house.

T. L. VAUGHN.
"The Champion Tobacco Manuf'r."

Manufacturing had been conducted here to some extent prior to 1873 but T. L. Vaughn erected the first factory expressly for tobacco making in that year and has ever since held a prominent place in the trade. It was a business in which, in one form or another, he had been familiar since childhood, and he was adapted to make a success of his projected enterprise. His business during the years since intervening forcibly illustrates this fact. The old building is now occupied by Vaughn, Locket & Co. Mr. Vaughn erecting his present fine structure in the fall of 1883. It fronts

100 ft. on Oldtown street and is 150 ft. in depth, and, inclusive of the basement has five floors. In the arrangement of this factory the practical ideas of a practical man were embodied—and the result is completeness so far as we can judge.

The capacity of this factory is estimated at a million pounds per year, but the out-put thus far has not exceeded about one-half that amount. Mr. Vaughn's leading brands are the Broad Axe, Big Auger and Old Rover.

The market sought and obtained by Mr. Vaughn does not differ materially from that of most of the factories here. His customers are largely located in South Carolina, Georgia and Alabama. A growing trade is held in Tennessee and a very considerable business is being built up in Ohio. Nearly all of Mr. Vaughn's customers are jobbers—he has some trade among retailers, but it is relatively small, while it is equally true that no traveling salesmen are employed to reach either wholesale or retail patrons.

MODEL TOBACCO WORKS.
B. F. Hanes, Proprietor.

Perhaps no man in this place was better calculated to build a model factory than B. F. Hanes whose efforts led to the completion of a fine structure on Chestnut street early in 1886. A dozen year's prior experience, in the business with his brothers, P. H. & J. W. Hanes, had consummated his plans for a practical workshop, and no means was spared in making this factory convenient and complete in all its workings. The building is a brick structure 53x153 ft., and, including the garret, has five floors. It is thoroughly lighted and ventilated. A 50 horse engine and 40 horse boiler, of Richmond make, runs the machinery, which also has hydraulic attachments. This house makes a specialty of the finer grades of goods, and confines its business entirely to the jobbing trade.

The leading brands are Benjamin Franklin, Carolina's Favorite, Golden Chain, Our Senator and others. With the second year Mr. Hanes accepted his brother Phillip as a partner, but left the firm name unchanged. More than 150 hands find employment here, and the output of the establishment for its two first years aggregated about 750,000 pounds which was nearly all sold before the commencement of this season's work, paying in these two years a revenue of $60,000 to the Government for tobacco stamps. The Haneses are both practical business men in every sense of the word, and are reaping the merited reward of a well planned industrial enterprise.

BAILEY BROTHERS.
Plug and Twist Tobacconists.

Eight years ago M. D. and P. N. Bailey added another to the long list of tobacco factories in Winston. They were in earnest—had come here to stay—and in '82 erected their substantial brick building on Chestnut street, 50x136 ft., four stories, and fitted up with engines, boiler and all other needed appliances. The father of this firm was a manufacturer, and the Bailey Brothers had been in the business at Statesville a half-dozen years before removing to Winston in 1880. Some twelve or fifteen regular brands of plug and twist tobacco are made, besides special brands. Among the leading and best known of the regular brands are Natahala, Old Bob, Ellen Fisher, Planter's Choice, O. K., Clipper, Silver Moon, May Queen and Lilac; in brief, all sizes and shapes are made that the public calls for. The leaf is purchased in the Winston warehouses by M. D., who gives his special attention to that branch of the trade and office matters, while P. N. is general superintendent of the mechanical work. In this as with other well regulated factories every care is made to grade the goods satisfactorily to customers, which brings additional orders. About 150 hands are employed and the annual output is 300,000 pounds.

RED ELEPHANT TOBACCO W'KS.
H. H. Reynolds Proprietor.

It is foreign to the purpose of this pamphlet to laud private enterprises or their proprietors, but a more fruitful field for deserved encomiums than the above could not well be found. H. H. Reynolds was raised in the finest tobacco section of Virginia, and much of his time in boyhood was occupied in growing and handling the best grades, so that he is now classed among the best selectors in this region.

Ten years ago Mr. R. took up a residence at Winston, as he believed the Piedmont Belt produced tobaccos of the finest chewing qualities, and to this he largely attributes his success, as the product of his establishment gives entire satisfaction to the trade. His business was at first conducted in a rented house, but on account of the rapid increase in his trade he was forced, in 1885, to build and equip his present mammoth works which cost over $25,000, and of which we present a cut on a succeeding page. The furnishing is complete in all respects and the business has increased about tenfold during his ten years in Winston; the first year showing a total output of 38,000 pounds and last year requiring 441,167 pounds of tobacco besides over 70,000 pounds of licorice and sugar. He has a large trade in the South and is successfully competing in Baltimore and the northern markets. The brands are, Reynolds' Best, 12 in. 3½, Red Elephant, 9 in. 4's, Red Elephant 7's, Honey Dew, Peabody, City Talk, Excelsior, Reaper, Twin City, Honey Comb (3 ply twist) and others.

Mr. Reynold's chief manager has been with him since 1880 and his book-keeper since 1883, while many of his hands have remained in his employ since he came to Winston. The personal attention given by the proprietor to every detail of business, insures for this establishment a continuance of its well merited success.

LOCKETT VAUGHN & CO.
Manufacturers of Plug Tobaccos.

E. L. Lockett, originally from Yanceyville, N. C., came to this place from Danville, Va., where he had been manager of a leading factory for several years. He was with Brown Bros. for some time, Bitting & Whitaker two years, and came to this partnership in 84. L. A. Vaughn is a native of Stokes, and has been raised in the tobacco trade, having several years been manager for his brother, T. L. Vaugn. Follin Brothers, of Charleston, S. C., wholesale tobacconists, purchased an interest in the business a year since and are holding a large run on the goods of this manufactory throughout their field of trade. One of the brothers is an active partner in the Winston house. This establishment gives employment to from 150 to 200 hands, the building has a capacity of a half million pounds and the annual output in plug alone is nearly 300,000 pounds. The territory tributary to the factory constantly increases, and every indication points to growing prosperity for this enterprise.

The leading brands are, Limited, Red Meat, Our Peach, and Brown Jug, and the force of the establishment is principally employed in supplying the demands of the trade for these special brands.

W. A. WHITAKER.
"Lucille" and Other Tobaccos.

W. A. Whitaker is a native of Yadkin county, and has had a wide experience in handling tobacco. His factory, on the corner of Church and 5th street, was originally built for a leaf house, is 44x146, having five floors, and with recent additions, is thoroughly equipped throughout. He employs about 150 hands, and has a capacity of fully half million pounds annually.

Mr. Whitaker uses only the leaf grown in the Piedmont section of this state, believing that this is the finest tobacco in the world for chewing goods, and that its superiority is largely what has made the Twin-City tobaccos so rapidly acquire a wide reputation wherever introduced. He is an expert buyer, and in his famous "Lucille" claims to have a product that cannot be excelled. White Wings, Coronet, Zip, Golden Slipper, Twin-City, Empress, Dick Graves, Peach and Honey, Olive Branch and Otter of Roses are among the favorite brands of this establishment. Mr. Whitaker is a progressive citizen as well as tobacconist, and has done much for the school system of Winston-Salem. The elegant system of electric light which Winston has, its magnificent club room, and various other public enterprises are largely indebted to his fostering care.

BITTING & HAY.
Manufacturers of Plug and Twist.

J. A. Bitting, President of the First National Bank, was one of the heaviest purchasers of leaf in the Winston market for a year or two after the business commenced here. In 1876 Mr. Bitting engaged in the banking business, and subsequently commenced tobacco manufacturing as Bitting & Whitaker. A couple of years since W. J. Ellis & Son built and equipped, with improved machinery, a tobacco factory 50x120 feet, four stories and basement, on Cherry street. This property was purchased by the firm of Bitting & Hay, January, '87, and for the first year turned out nearly a quarter of a million pounds of plug and twist. It has a capacity for double that amount, and is running about 150 hands. The product is principally sold in the southern states, and their leading brand is the Zebra, although several other popular styles are made. W. S. Hay, the junior partner, is a native of Rockingham county, and came to Winston in 1880. He was employed with Bitting & Whitaker until accepting an interest as partner in the above enterprise. Mr. Hay is thoroughly conversant with the requirements of the trade. Mr. Bitting is an old tobacconist, and there can be no question as to the solidity and success of this comparatively new firm in Winston.

W. W. WOOD & CO.,
Belew's Creek Street, Salem.

Located just in the edge of Salem, this firm gets its mail from the Winston postoffice, thus illustrating how closely the two places are bound together, and the appropriateness of the cognomen, Twin-City. Mr. Wood is a native of Virginia, residing in this state from boyhood, and was for many years engaged in merchandising and manufacturing tobacco in Surry county. Ten years ago he located in Winston, but in 1882 he had his factory burned, and for two subsequent years was connected with Brown & Bro. In 1885 Mr. Wood, in company with E. A. Ebert, a former merchant, and Dr. H. T. Bahnson, both Salemites, occupied the present fine four-story brick, 50x107 feet, and which is thoroughly equipped for every demand of their trade. This establishment uses about a quarter of a million pounds of leaf yearly, the product being more largely sold in Georgia than any other state. "Maud Muller" is a special favorite, while any style of plug and twist is made to meet the demands of trade. It has steam equipments, and gives employment to over 100 hands.

OGBURN HILL & CO.,
Manufacturers of Plug Tobacco.

The firm of Ogburn, Hill & Co., was

formed 10 years ago by C. J. Ogburn, a native of this county, who had been raised in tobacco manufacturing, and W. P. Hill, of Stokes county, formerly in business for some time. The enterprise was conducted on Old Town street until 1884, when the requirements of their trade demanded better accommodations.— January 1st of that year C. D. Ogburn was admitted, a new brick, 45x120 ft. five floors, was erected on Cherry street, and occupied in November, 1884. Some of the favorite brands are O. H. & Co's Choice, Dixie, Gold Leaf, Winston Leader, Eagle, Minnie Ogburn, Drummer and others. Mr. C. J. Ogburn attends to the buying and prizing, and Mr. Hill to the classing of leaf. The office is principally in the hands of C. D. Ogburn, and by this division of labor among the copartners the best and most practical results are obtained.

The specialties of the firm are fine and fancy 12 in-3's, for which they have a large demand.

About 100 hands are employed and over 200,000 pounds of leaf handled yearly.

HODGIN BROTHERS & LUNN.
Plug and Twist Tobacco.

Messrs. Payne, Lunn & Morris erected one of the fine large factories on Cherry street which were built in 1884. The size of this structure is 50x135 feet, four stories in height. Messrs. Payne and Morris withdrew from the firm, and L. L. Lunn, in company with J. M. and G. D. Hodgin, formed the present firm with this year. The new partnership employs over 100 hands, and expect to turn out 200,000 pounds or more of manufactured product. Mr. Lunn is from Salisbury, and the Hodgin brothers natives of this place, J. M. having been raised in the tobacco business, and G. D. has been for the past half dozen years connected with the First National bank of Winston. This factory is by 15 feet the largest of the Big Five, and its output is a material assistance in swelling the aggregate of the Twin City tobacco transactions.

BLACKBURN, DALTON & CO.,
Manufacturers of Plug and Twist.

Organized in 1883, this firm erected their large factory on Cherry street—one of the Big Five—a year later. It is 50x116 feet, four stories, and with the usual equipments. Samuel Blackburn is a Stokes county man, and was in manufacturing there prior to coming to Winston five years since. R. E. Dalton is also from Stokes, and as his father was a manufacturer, he was raised in the tobacco business. Buck Ellington, of Rockingham, who has been a tobacco salesman for a dozen years past is the "Co." The brands of this house are Cora Moore, Come Again, Ben Hill, Bob Vance, and a score of others. The firm employs over 100 hands, and their annual purchases of leaf is about a quarter of a million pounds.

BYNUM & COTTEN.
Plug and Twist Tobaccos.

The members of this firm—Taylor Bynum and Rod Cotten—are both natives of Chatham county, and were engaged in tobacco manufacturing at Hillsboro prior to removing to Winston in 1879. Five years later the firm erected the fine four-story brick factory at the corner of Cherry and 6th streets. This is 50x122, properly equipped, and about 100 busy workers here find employment, turning out the usual product of other houses with like number of hands. Mr. Bynum has long made a special study of leaf purchases, and attends to that department, while Mr. Cotten has the superintendency of the manufactory. The demand for their product has been good, and last season's manufacture was disposed of some time since. The leading brands are Wachovia,

T. Bynum's Extra Fine Pounds, Silver Wave, Mary Lee, Red Man, Nashville Chew, Smart Alex, and others.

S. A. OGBURN.
Plug and Twist Tobacco.

One of the earliest tobacco manufacturers of this section was the venerable Jas. E. Ogburn, father of the above, who commenced making plug about 1850, in a small way, at the Ogburn homestead some four miles out of Winston. In 1855 the capacity of the works was increased, and for five succeeding years the output was ten to twenty thousand lbs. annually. The raw material for this being raised by the neighbors within a radius of a few miles around.

After the war S. A. Ogburn, who had formerly superintended his father's works, was for a year with Col. J. W. Alspaugh, and in 1878 was one of the firm of Ogburn, Hill & Co. Subsequently retiring from this firm and in 1885 opened up business at the corner of 7th and Old Town Sts. He has employed about 60 hands here, making an annual output of over 60,000 pounds, but his trade demands better accommodations and Mr. O. is now building a brick factory on 7th street near the R. R., which will be 54x75 ft., four stories and have a capacity of over a quarter of a million pounds.

R. L. CANDLER & CO..
Plug and Twist Tobaccos.

R. L. Candler is a native of Lynchburg, Va., and came to Winston in 1883. In 1885 Mr. S. B. Zigler opened up a factory on 4½ street in a brick structure which he had previously erected, 40x100 feet, and four stories. Three years later Mr. Candler came in as a partner, and subsequently succeeded to the entire business, continuing the firm title as above. When in full operation Mr. Candler employs about 100 hands, and uses in his manufactory about 40,000 pounds of leaf per month. The favorite brands of this institution are Bonny Jean, Rebel Boy, Red Seal, Derby, Pansy Blossom, Carnival, Casino, Veto, Jubilee, and Blue Stockings, which are sold to the jobbing trade of the south. Mr. Candler was one of the prime movers in organizing the Twin City club, and is a young man of progressive spirit.

H. SCALES & CO..
Manufacturers of Plug.

Major Hamilton Scales was the first tobacco manufacturer in Winston, commencing his work in 1870 in a carriage house on Liberty street, and building his present establishment in the centennial year. Prior to opening up business in Winston Major Scales had been making plug tobacco in Stokes county for a few years, having before the war been engaged in the business in his native county—Rockingham. With the present season T. J. and N. S. Wilson, Winstonian tobacconists, have been added to the firm, and will doubtless give to it a new impetus. T. J. Wilson has for several years past been with N. D. Sullivan, while N. S. Wilson, as book-keeper at Farmer's warehouse, has secured an intimate knowledge of the weed. The prominent brands are Alex Stevens, Bob Toombs, Ida Bryan, Spanker, and Rabbit Gum.

C. HAMLEN & SONS.
Plug and Smoking Tobaccos.

A native of Pearson county, N. C., Mr. Hamlen began the manufacture of tobacco at Roxboro in 1869, and five years later moved to the Twin City. He built the largest factory of Winston in 1874, and subsequently made considerable additions, but a number of the factories of more recent date have surpassed Mr. Hamlin in capacity, architecture and elegance of equipments. In the spring of 1887 his sons, M. S. and C. P., were admitted as partners in the concern.

and have added the vigor of youth to the experience of age in the firm. In smoking brands the favorites are Powhattan and Volunteer, while the plug styles are Pride of Carolina, Acme, Belle of Winston, Sunny South, and several others. The house is one of the established enterprises of Winston, and well known in the southern tobacco trade.

J. A. BUTNER,
Plug, Twist and Smoking Tobacco.

Dr. J. A. Butner established his present business in 1885, just in the edge of Salem, but receives his business mail at Winston. The building is 50x116 feet, four stories, and has a capacity for more than a quarter million pounds of manufactured tobacco, but Mr. Butner finds it quite as profitable to supply the demands of his trade by purchasing from the country factories when they are disposed to sell at close margins; consequently he does quite an extensive jobbing trade. Mr. B. is a native of Salem, but residing in Indiana from 1858 to 1881, when he returned to his native home.

W. T. GRAY & CO.,
Granulated Smoking Tobacco.

Capt. W. T. Gray and Watt Martin, his partner, are both natives of Winston. Mr. Martin being the traveling salesman, and Capt. Gray the managing partner at the factory. The manufacture of smoking goods requires but few employees, and this firm, with less than 15 hands on an average will probably turn out 75,000 pounds of the favorite brands. Off duty is put up in attractive style—3 oz. red and blue pouches—and Gray's Winston is made from selected leaf of rich bright color, with strict regard to cleanliness and uniformity. A new style for either smoking or chewing is made from cut plug and known as square knot. The raw supplies are all secured in this city, and with a building 40x70, of four floors, W. T. Gray & Co. have one of the best exclusive smoking tobacco factories here.

S. BYERLY & SON,
Smoking Tobaccos and Groceries.

This firm started in the Grocery trade of North Liberty street, Winston, some ten years ago, and four years since began the manufacture of smoking tobacco. They give employment to about ten hands, and many thousand pounds of their Eagle brand smoking have been sold throughout Georgia, South Carolina and other Southern States. More recently it is gaining a wide reputation in Pennsylvania. The firm, although not claiming to be classed among our largest manufacturers, has an honorable record and is increasing its trade from year to year, in both the merchandise and manufacturing departments.

T. F. LEAK,
Manufacturer of Smoking Tobacco.

T. F. Leak was raised in the tobacco trade, his father having been a manufacturer in Stokes county. Mr. Leak started the first smoking tobacco business in Winston, seventeen years ago, and still continues as a manufacturer, having in the meantime sent out many thousand pounds of his goods to dealers in the South. His brands of Southern Belle and Wide Awake are widely known among smokers. Mr. Leak purchases all his stock in the Winston markets.

CIGAR FACTORY.
I. LEOPOLD'S
Winston Cigar Manufactory.

Born in the Empire City, I. Leopold was for ten years employed at the cigar trade in New York before he came to Winston. Five years ago he engaged with V. O. Thompson & Co., as manager and superintendent, and a year or two since, believing there was a field for the business here, he opened up cigar making on his own account, and since the retirement of his former employers has the entire field to himself. In 1887, his first year of manufacturing, the output showed 532,000 cigars of which a half million had been sold at the end of the year, and the indications are that the trade of 1888 will double this record. Mr. Leopold is full of enterprise, has equipped his factory with modern cigar machinery, and employs about 20 hands. He occupies every foot of space over the entire length of the Winston Postoffice building, and with his present rate of increase will doubtless be compelled to erect a large factory two or three years hence. The men who are liberal with printer's ink and furnish reliable goods to their customers, seldom fail of success; and one thing which speaks highly for this house is the fact that a large majority of our local dealers have found it to their interest to patronize him. Mr. Leopold has a good trade over the Carolinas and is reaching out for business into Georgia, Alabama, Tennessee and Florida. His standard 10 cent goods are Henry Clay, John C. Calhoun and Iron Prince. In 5 cent brands, Leopold's Havanas take the lead, while Twin-City, Maggie Brown, Our Chum, Pine Logs, Zebra, North State Belle, Leopold's Ponies and a score of other brands are made. Success to the Winston Cigar Manufactory.

LEAF AND STEM DEALERS.

M. N. WILLIAMSON.

Leaf Tobacco and Stem Broker.

The standard market value of tobacco in Winston is largely maintained by our leaf dealers, and their regular attendance at the market with the manufacturers creates a steady and permanent demand for all grades of goods. M. N. Williamson is a Virginian, 14 years in Winston, and for ten years past in the leaf trade. His business made a rapid increase and in 1881 he erected the large factory on Old Town Street, 40x90, four stories. This is fitted with the Triumph Sumner heat system, which plan retains the flavor and toughness, and Mr. W. has a large number of customers in the Northwest who recognize the superiority of North Carolina tobacco for flavor, color, and chewing qualities. The average annual output is a million pounds, nearly half of which is shipped to Europe. Employment is given to 20 or 30 hands, and this is entitled to rank among our largest leaf tobacco firms.

J. B. MOSELEY.

Tobacco Leaf Dealer.

J. B. Moseley is a Virginian, and was for some years engaged in the tobacco business in Danville. He is an expert buyer, and when the markets are low is ready to purchase, recure, sort and hold the goods until the manufacturers or distant customers need the product at an advanced figure. Mr. Moseley has been doing business in a rented house on 4½ St., but is now adding to his capacity as well as to the architectural beauty of our city by erecting a four story brick 40x90 on Cherry street, fronting the Big Five factories. Every permanent addition to the Winston manufactories is deserving of recognition, and Mr. Moseley will doubtless receive a just business reward for his enterprise.

A. A. SMITH & CO.,

Leaf Tobacco Dealers.

A. A. Smith is a native of Lynchburg, Va., and came to Winston about a dozen years since. He engaged in the tobacco leaf trade, and was subsequently a partner with M. N. Williamson, as one of the firm of Williamson and Smith. Later Mr. Smith engaged with R. J. Reynolds, our well known tobacco manufacturer, in his present enterprise, making the firm name of A. A. Smith & Co. The Butner factory is used by the new firm for storage and prizing rooms, and this leaf house does a fair share of trade in that line. The specialty of the firm is N. C. bright mahogany wrappers, which from their fine texture and rich body, are eagerly sought for by western and northern dealers.

M. W. NORFLEET & SON.,
Dealers in Tobacco Leaf.

M. W. Norfleet has for several years past operated as a leaf dealer, and three years since accepted as a partner in that department his son, Jas. K. The firm have a brick factory 35x80 feet, with four floors, on 3rd street, and have a capacity for handling a million pounds of leaf annually, which is principally sold to the export trade.

COLEMAN BROTHERS.
Leaf Dealers and Brokers.

The Coleman Brothers are from Halifax county, Va., and came to Winston in Nov., 1884 to engage in the tobacco trade. Their principal purchases are of such colors or grades as are used least in the Winston manufactories, thus assisting in giving a staple value to such kinds of tobacco as would be dull in this market.

B. J. SHEPPARD & CO.,
Leaf Tobacco Dealers.

B. J. Sheppard is a native of Richmond, Va., and in the tobacco business continuously since the war, having been in Winston for the past dozen years. In 1883 he built the large factory at the corner of 4th and Chestnut streets, 50x90 and four stories, which is fitted with all the steam drying attachments.

EDMUNDS & GILMER.
Tobacco Leaf Dealers.

E. C. Edmunds of Halifax county, Va., came to Winston some 5 years ago to engage in the leaf trade, and a couple of years since associated with himself Capt. Gilmer under the above title. The firm occupy the Shaffner factory in Salem as a leaf house, getting their mail at Winston.

F. G. SCHAUM,
Buyer for Marburg Bros., of Balto.,

Has been many years in the business, and thoroughly understands the values and grades of leaf. He first came to Winston in 1875, was sent to other markets for a time, but returned to this city five years ago, and makes heavy purchases for the above house.

There are one or two other leaf firms, and a score of "pin hookers" who purchase on speculation, from the planters direct. So the tobacco trade is well represented in all departments.

ADJACENT FACTORIES.
REYNOLDS BROS.,
Centerville—Winston P. O.

One mile Southeast from the Salem Post-office, in the suburb of Centerville is found the Reynolds Brothers tobacco factory which was erected in 1883. It is 40x157 feet, two and four stories in height, having an extension of 40 feet for the boiler, engine and box manufactory. The Reynolds Brothers, C. A. and T. E. are natives of Rockingham county, and have been in the tobacco business for fifteen years. They employ over 100 hands and the annual product approximates 200,000 pounds. The Reynolds Bros. are young men of push and enterprise, have a fine dairy farm adjoining the factory, and a private water-works system connected with the establishment, which furnishes pure spring water to all parts of the factory. Hose attachments for fire protection have been made on every floor, and the establishment is thoroughly equipped throughout for plug, twist and smoking products. The leading brands are, Reynolds Brothers' Best, Fruit of the Farm, Minnie Reynolds, Little Pearl and Old Ratler. In smoking, their leader is Top Notch. Careful selection, good business tact and persevering industry have brought a large trade to the Reynolds Bros.

S. J. NISSEN.
Waughtown—Salem P. O.

The name of Nissen is well known in the Twin-City, and the suburb of Waughtown with her thousand industrious inhabitants, almost owes her existence to the varied enterprises of the Nissen Bros. S. J. Nissen was formerly in the wagon business with his brothers, but in 1885 built a tobacco factory, and has since been engaged in the manufacture of plug and smoking tobaccos. The Nissen factory does not yet rank among the largest industries of this section, but every care is taken to properly select the grades and to give as close margins to customers as establishments doing a larger trade. The leading brands are S. & W., Buncombe, Slim Jim, and in Smoking, Old Solid Comfort. Mr. Nissen should have the hearty co-operation of Waughtown people for continued success in this enterprise, which gives employment to many hands who are not versed in mechanical arts.

SULLIVAN FACTORY.
WALKERTOWN, N. C.

There are a number of substantial tobacco factories in this county, all of which go to build up the interests of the Twin-City, as most of them purchase their supplies from our tobacco warehouses and spend a fair share of their profits in the Twin-City. One especially deserving mention in these columns is that which is in successful operation at Walkertown, under the proprietorship of N. D. Sullivan. Mr. S. is a native of this county, has had thirty years experience in handling tobacco, and the excellency of Sullivan's Best, and Sullivan's Free and Easy plug has acquired for it a wide reputation among lovers of the weed. Mr. Sullivan commenced in an unpretentious manner but has added to his facilities until he now has a well equipped establishment and manufactures about 150,000 pounds of high grade tobaccos each year.

The county has several other factories and there are three or four tobacco firms in Winston that are omitted by request, or from other reasons not necessary to explain.

RED ELEPHANT TOBACCO WORKS.
[See page 37.]

PUBLIC BENEFITS.

RAILROADS.
RICHMOND & DANVILLE LINE.

Fifty years ago the aggregate railroads of America measured less than 250 miles and required about 1,000 employees. Ten years later it had grown to 7,000 miles, 5,000 employees, and $200,000,000 of capital. To-day there is more than 150,000 miles of iron highway in the United States, the year just past having shown a construction record of 12,524 miles, which is greater than any preceding 12 months. Nearly a billion of dollars is now invested in railroad enterprises, and 750,000 hands required for its operation. All other agencies combined are overshadowed when compared with what railroads have done in the development of our country, as every mile of road is estimated to bring 20,000 acres of land into feasible culture, raise its value 100 per cent., and add immensely to the wealth of the country through which it traverses.

The Northwestern North Carolina Railroad was built from Greensboro to this place in 1872, and first opened Winston-Salem to the world. A few years later it became a portion of the R. & D. System which gave the Twin-City direct communication with the metropolitan cities of the east.

The Richmond and Danville Railroad comprises 2,400 miles of line in operation, and the extension of the road from here to Wilkesboro, is now being vigorously prosecuted, and we hope will soon open communications with the rich agricultural districts which lie between here and the mountains. The general offices of the system are at Washington, D. C., Geo. S. Scott, President; E. B. Thomas, General Manager; and Jas. L. Taylor, as General Passenger Agent. The R. & D. is fully recognized as one of the important railroad systems of America.

WESTERN UNION TELEGRAPH.

The W. U. Telegraph started here in 1884 and the present manager of the Winston office came here with the first of this year. J. M. Pendleton is a native of Virginia, began telegraphy a dozen years ago and thoroughly understands the business. The office is in the Gray block, is fitted with automatic protectors and has through connections with Richmond, Washington, Raleigh, and Charlotte. This is a money transfer office and its cable business is quite large, in consequence of the leaf dealers business on the continent.

HISTORY, HOTELS, ETC.

Doubtless the oldest hotel in this section of country is the Salem Tavern. The first Inn of the place was burned in 1781, and two or three years later the old brick portion of the Salem Hotel was erected which, although it has endured the ravages of more than a hundred years is still a substantial structure. Four years ago this property was purchased, as a residence, by Dr. Z. Swift, of Florida, who came here to secure for his daughters the advantages of the Academy. We visited the room which President Washington occupied while stopping at this place in 1791, and from which he penned the following reply, June 1st, 1791, (the original of which is still preserved in the archives of the church here) in response to a letter of welcome from the Moravian Brethren:

"*To the United Brethren, of Wachovia:*—GENTLEMEN:—I am greatly indebted to your respectful and affectionate expression of personal regard and I am not less obliged by the patriotic sentiment contained in your address.

From a society whose governing principles are industry and the love of order, much may be expected towards the improvement and prosperity of the country in which their settlements are formed, and experience authorizes the belief that much will be obtained.

Thanking you with grateful sincerity for your prayers in my behalf, I desire to assure you of my best wishes for your social and individual happiness.
G. WASHINGTON.

THE HOME.—Under the head of Societies, etc., we should have called attention to the Salem Home for aged and infirmed people and orphan children, which is supported by charitable ladies, organized in societies of ten each and known as the King's Daughters. A building has been purchased on Main Street, which is under the supervision of a matron and has accommodations for over 30 occupants.

GOD'S ACRE.—The Moravian burying ground is known as God's Acre, and is admirable from its simplicity. The graves are made in parallel rows, which are intersected at intervals by alleys that divide the plat into blocks. Children are buried in one apartment, sisters in another, and men in a third. No mark of distinction in granite spire or costly sculptured marble is allowed, but a simple marble block with inscription, placed flat upon the head of each grave. The oldest grave is marked 1770, and since then more than a thousand others have been interred side by side, all now covered by a grassy lawn and shaded by cedars of a century's growth. Cedar Alley in front of this sacred spot, is canopied on both sides by the o'er-spreading cedar spires, and is one of the handsomest and pleasantest walks in the city.

The Cemetery.—Crossing a ravine to the eastward from the above, is found among the original forest trees the peoples' cemetery. This has a number of handsome monuments, and could be made an attractive spot, but as yet has had little care bestowed upon its surroundings. Those having the matter in charge would do well to spend a little more towards beautifying this sacred spot.

The Mineral Spring, on Marshall Street, produces a most excellent chalybeate water and it is singular that more persistent effort should not have been taken to advertise this acknowledged fountain of health-giving properties. A good place for a sanitarium and the right man should take hold of the matter at once and erect a suitable building for the application of natures remedies.

The Twin-City is deficient in the matter of a first-class hotel. Every progressive city that expects to succeed, and especially in the South, should have its tourist home, kept in unexceptionable style, where those who can and will pay fancy rates, may secure every needed comfort. A house of that kind, in this place, with a hundred rooms or more, could be easily filled a large part of the year; as the elevation, salubrity and healthfulness would attract large numbers if we had superb accommodations.

Hotel Fountain and Merchants, the two largest hotels of this place, are under one management and have, combined, more than 50 rooms. W. R. Vickers, the lessee, is a native of Durham and was for several years a landlord at Reidsville. He is known as the portly man of Winston, raising the scale beam above 350 pounds. R. Harris, the Clerk, is popular with the commercial travelers and the guests in general.

Terry House is in the new Starbuck Block, and is conducted by the affable Mrs. N. J. Terry. This house contains only 16 rooms, but is constantly filled with guests to its full capacity, as the rates given and the board furnished seem to fully satisfy the requirements of the boarders. Mrs. Terry is attentive to the requirements of her guests, has kept boarders in Winston for seven years, and is to be congratulated on her success as a landlady.

BUILDINGS AND OFFICIALS.

INTERNAL REVENUE.

A branch office of the Fifth Internal Revenue District is kept in the First National Bank building, under the management of D. D. Shelton, with Mrs. F. G. Hellen assistant. Nothing but tobacco and cigar stamps is sold and yet the books show that the receipts for six months prior to January 1st, 1888, aggregated $277,- 618.90, all handled and accounted for by two persons, with a cost of less than one per cent. to the Government for collecting. This will also give to our readers some idea of the immense tax taken from the people of the tobacco growing and manufacturing districts of North Carolina, —this place alone sending more than half a million dollars annually to the U. S. Treasury.

COUNTY OFFICERS AND BUILDINGS.

The Act forming Forsyth county was passed in 1848 and the deed for

51¾ acres, at $256.25, was made by Chas. F. Kluge on behalf of the Moravian church land department, to Francis Fries, chairman of the board of the county court, May 12, 1849. This plat covered only from 1st to 7th streets, between Church street on the east, and the parallel of Old Town street on the west. The county site was officially named Winston by an Act of the Legislature passed Jan. 15th, 1851.

The court house was built in 1851-2 and prior to this, court was held in Concert Hall, Salem. The old court house and old jail cost about $10,000 and served the purpose quite well at first, but the changes of 36 years have made an incalculable difference in the city and county, the old court house is entirely inadequate —a disgrace to the enterprise of the the Twin-City—should be torn down and replaced by an edifice that would be commodious and an advertisement to the progressive spirit of this section of country.

The Present Jail was built in 1885 at a cost of over $12,000 and is a handsome, safe and commodious structure. It has five iron cells, manufactured by the Hall Safe and Lock Co., of Cincinnati. These cells each have five hammocks for prisoners and a room on an upper floor has been planned for as many more. J. W. Bradford, of Granville county, formerly chief-of-police here, has been jailor for a year or two past and has safely handled several hundred prisoners.

Sheriffs.—William Flint was elected first Sheriff of Forsyth county. He was succeeded by Mathias Masten, J. G. Hill, Augustus Fogle and the present incumbent, John Boyer is a native of the county and in agricultural pursuits prior to his election in 1883 to the office of Sheriff. Mr. Boyer was re-elected in '85 and has made a satisfactory record. His deputy is W. J. Cooper, of Salem, who was for twenty years in the milling business.

Clerks of Court.—John C. Blum was appointed by Judge Settle, the first clerk of courts, and was succeeded by John Blackburn who held the office for a quarter of a century. C. S. Hauser, the present Clerk of the Superior Court, was born in this vicinity, served a time as county commissioner, four years as Register, and has now been Clerk for a dozen years. He is assisted by R. W. Nading, who has recently graduated from the Graded Schools.

A. J. Stafford was first County Clerk and served many years under the old form of government. Francis Fries was first Clerk and Master of the Court of Equity. Judge T. J. Wilson was first County Solicitor, and was succeeded by Col. Joseph Masten.

Registers of Deeds.—F. C. Meinung first officiated as Register of Deeds and the office was subsequently held by C. L. Rights, H. S. Belt, N. S. Cook, C. S. Hauser, J. H. White, Jr., and D. P. Mast. Capt. Mast is a native of Watanga county, and has been 18 years in Winston. He was admitted to the bar Jan. '68, served as engrossing clerk of the N. C. Senate, 1870-1, enrolling clerk of the General Assembly '74-5, was Mayor of Winston during the Centennial year, and in Dec. 76 became Register of Deeds, which office he continues to hold. The Captain does an office practice in law, giving special attention to the settlement of estates and other matters closely allied to the court house offices. K. S. Lott, of Salem, has officiated as Deputy Register for several years.

By virtue of his office as Register, Capt. Mast is Clerk of the Board of County Commissioners. A. E. Conrad, of Vienna, Chairman of the same; J. W. Fries, of Salem, and N. W. Sapp, of Kernersville, make up the board.

County Treasurers.—Geo. Linville, Robert Linville and Wm. Barrow, were County Trustees under the old system of County government. Robt.

Linville was the first County Treasurer elected by the people, and was succeeded by C. J. Ogburn, who held several terms. R. L. Cox, the present incumbent is a native of Forsyth County, and was engaged in farming prior to his election as county treasurer in 1883. He was elected again in '85 and is acceptably serving the last year of his second term—his books having always been found correct.

SALEM OFFICIALS, ETC.

Mayor.—Christian Fogle, father of Augustus Fogle, the Mayor of Salem, located "way out in the country," near the site of the present Twin-City depot, in 1814. The place is now in Winston and the Mayor was born here in 1820. Mr. Fogle learned cabinet making and before settling down in life spent several years in going with wagons to the "far west," beyond the Mississippi. He was for 20 years Steward at the Academy, has served Salem as Mayor 9 years before this, was for 6 years county Sheriff, and has made a long and honored record in active life.

Other Officials.—L. N. Clinard has for over 20 years officiated as treasurer and clerk of the board. The Board of Commissioners are H. E. Fries, H. W. Shore, S. E. Butner, H. S. Crist, H. McIver, A. A. Spaugh and A. C. Vogler. Policeman, Samuel Ebert; Lamp Lighter, Romulus Tesh.

WINSTON AND ITS OFFICIALS.

Incorporation.—By Act of the Legislature, Winston was made an incorporated village in Feb. 1859. At that time the bounds of the county seat were extended from the old 51¼ acres to reach 1278 ft. west from the court house, and a sufficient distance east to make the plat a half mile wide and northward one-half mile from the court house. Subsequently the plat has been enlarged to 1¼ mile from east to west, south to Salem boundary and northward one mile from the court house.

Mayors.—Wm. Barrow was the first Mayor after the incorporation of Winston, and as the town books up to 1879 have been lost or destroyed we have labored under considerable difficulty to get the exact order of succession, but we think the following is nearly correct: P. A. Wilson, J. W. Alspaugh, T. J. Wilson, H. K. Thomas, Jacob Tise, T. T. Best, J. W. Alspaugh, D. P. Mast, Martin Grogan, A. B. Gorrell, 1879–'80–'81, P. A. Wilson, '82, J. C. Buxton, '83–'84, S. H. Smith, '85, T. J. Wilson, '86, Chas. Buford, '87–'88. Chas. Buford is a Virginian, and came to Winston in 1875, as Agent of the R. & D. Railroad at this place, which position he still fills acceptably. Mayor Buford served out the unexpired term of S. H. Smith, who resigned when appointed as Postmaster, was elected as Mayor in '87, and re-elected to this honorable office a few weeks since.

Secretaries.—Those who have officiated as Secretaries and Treasurers during the past ten years are, G. W. Hinshaw, Jas. H. Gray, J. H. Masten, R. B. Kerner, S. H. Hodgin, P. A. Wilson, E. H. Wilson, the present incumbent, who is a native of Winston and son of Judge Wilson and partner in the Orinoco Warehouse.

Town Commissioners.—The Commissioners of Winston are J. A. Gray, P. N. Bailey, R. E. Dalton, Joel Jacobs, J. M. Byerly, J. W. Alspaugh, and E. H. Wilson.

Tax Collector and Constable.—J. C. Bessent, of Davie County, was elected to the office of City Tax Collector and Constable in 1882 and has filled the office so acceptably as to still hold his place. Lieutenant Bessent is well informed about city matters in general, and the historian is indebted to him for many valuable historical facts.

Police Force.—J. A. Meroney is a native of Davie County, and was on the force a year or two before his election as chief. This town being a manufacturing place has many transient negroes and really needs a larger force than the present. A. Stewart is from Rockingham County, and has now been on the force for four years. N. D. Dowdy is from Chatham County, and several years in the service, while J. P. Penry is from Davie County, and has done efficient work for a year or two past. The Winston policemen are prompt, brave and energetic; but hardly sufficient for the work on hand.

Sanitary Police.—N. W. Nading, an old resident of this place, has recently been appointed as sanitary policeman, but we believe the general health and good of the city would be enhanced by placing a competent medical man in charge. No false economy should prevent the best possible sanitation of a growing city, as its future largely depends upon wise regulations in this respect.

PROFESSIONAL, ETC.

LEGAL FRATERNITY.

The Bar of Winston has ever had, and still retains a fair share of able lawyers. Judge D. H. Starbuck and Col. Joseph Masten, deceased, were among the first in practice here. Hon. T. J. Wilson was born in Stokes county (now Forsyth) in 1815, admitted to the practice of law in '41 and in '47 erected the brick house diagonally across Main Street, from the Orinoco Warehouse, which was the first house built in the original plat of Winston. The Judge was the first attorney of this city and still continues in the profession. He was elected Judge in 1874, but from some irregularity in the time of holding the election, officiated on the bench only six months. Judge Wilson has been Mayor several times.

Hon. A. H. Sheppard practiced at this bar between his terms in Congress. Col. J. W. Alspaugh was admitted in 1857 and practiced for ten years after the war.

WATSON & BUXTON.

Attorneys and Insurance Agents.

Hon. C. B. Watson is a native of Forsyth county and after the usual preparations, began the practice of law in 1870. In 1880 he was Senator from the 32d district of N. C. and has made a prominent record both in practice and in politics.

Hon. J. C. Buxton is a native of Asheville, graduated at Trinity College, of Hartford, Conn., read law in Geneva, N. Y. and was admitted to practice in January, 1875. He was Mayor of Winston in 1883-4, resigning on his last term to be elected to the State Senate of which body he was an honored member in '85. Mr. Buxton was a delegate to the National Convention at Chicago in 1884 and his name has been prominently mentioned as a candidate for Congress at the coming election. The firm of Watson & Buxton was formed in 1885 and occupies rooms in the First National Bank building. Besides doing a large law practice they write insurance for the Royal, of Liverpool, London and Lancashire, Phoenix and Orient, of Hartford; Fire Association, of Philadelphia; Germania and Underwriters, of N. Y. The Norwich Union and Georgia Home. In life insurance the old reliable Mutual Life of New York is represented.

GLENN & GLENN.

Fourth Street, Opp. Court House.

W. B. Glenn, the senior partner of the above firm, is a native of Yadkin County, graduated from Princeton, N. J., read law under Chief Justice Pearson, and was admitted to the bar in 1872. He practiced in Yadkin for a time, and was for many years a partner in the firm of Watson & Glenn. He was a member of the Legislature in 1874, Democratic elector in '76, and in '84 served again in the General Assembly.

R. B. Glenn is from Rockingham County, attended Davidson College, the University of Virginia, subsequently read law under the instructions of Chief Justice Pearson, and was admitted to practice ten years ago. He was sent to the Legislature from Stokes County in 1881, was Democratic elector in '84, and was Solicitor for the 9th Judicial district, in 1886–'87. The alliance of Glenn & Glenn was formed in 1885, and the firm practices in all the adjacent Courts.

ELLER & STARBUCK,
Attorneys at Law.

Judge D. H. Starbuck practiced law here from the time Winston was made a county seat until his death a year ago. A. H. Eller was born in Wilkes county, reared in Ashe, received the degree of A. B. from the N. C. University in 1885, read law with George N. Folk, of Caldwell county and after his admittance in '86, entered the office of Judge Starbuck.

H. R. Starbuck graduated from the State University at Chapel Hill, in '87, was admitted to practice within the present year, and has recently formed a partnership with Mr. Eller. The new firm have the law library which Judge Starbuck accumulated during his long practice, and are just arranging to make large additions. The firm do a general insurance business, representing the St. Paul Fire & Marine, Washington and Connecticut Mutual Life and other reliable Companies. Special attention given to collections, negotiation of loans, sale of land and management of estates.

R. B. KERNER.
Attorney—Bitting Block.

Born in Kernersville, R. B. Kerner, after the common schools, attended the University at Chapel Hill, and taught for four years in the Salem Boys' School prior to his majority. He then attended Dick & Dillard's law school at Greensboro, was admitted to the bar, and in '83 was appointed as Solicitor for the Inferior Court, officiating there until that Court was abolished. Mr. Kerner, although a young man, has been City Clerk and Treasurer, and on both the Board of City and School Commissioners. He has a good library and convenient office rooms in the Bitting block.

E. E. GRAY.
Attorney and Insurance Agent.

Eugene E. Gray is a native of Winston, and was educated at Emory & Henry College, Va. He attended Judge Strong's law school, of Raleigh, was admitted to the bar here in Jan. 1879, and has since continued to practice in this place. Mr. Gray's rooms are over Wachovia National Bank, and in addition to a general law and commercial practice he also writes insurance. Mr. Gray has taken special pains to accept none but reliable Companies, and he represents several leading ones in this and the old country.

J. S. GROGAN.
One Door South of Vaughn & Pepper.

J. S. Grogan is a native of Rockingham county, and came to Winston in 1873. He took a literary course at Bingham's School, attended Dick & Dillard's law school at Greensboro, was admitted to the bar here in '84, and has since been in the practice of law in Winston. His office is up stairs, next door to Vaughn & Pepper's store, where he does a general practice.

L. J. WILLIAMS.
Attorney and Counsellor.

Lewis J. Williams was born in Yadkin, and is a son of Nicholas L. Williams, who was well known throughout the State, and died a couple of years since, aged 86. His father, Col. Jos. Williams, of Revolutionary note, was one of the pioneers of Western N. C., settling at Panther Creek, prior to the war with the mother country. L. J. Williams who resided on the old homestead, was burned out March '85, and desiring to secure better educational advantages for his family, moved to Winston. He read law with different members of the Bar of this place, and was recently admitted to practice, having office rooms in the Bitting block.

E. A. GRIFFITH.
Over Clark & Ford's Store.

E. A. Griffith is a native of this county, took a literary course at Chapel Hill, was admitted to practice Oct. '84, and has since been in practice in Winston. Mr. Griffith gives special attention to the collection of claims, and negotiates loans on good security.

There are some other attorneys, and a half dozen magistrates which we have not had time to interview, and we have no further space to devote to legal matters.

MEDICAL FRATERNITY.

Salem has had a long and able list of medical advisers. Dr. Schuman and the senior Dr. Keehln practiced for many years, and two of its prominent physicians, Drs. A. T. Zevely and T. F. Keehln, left the stage of action about a dozen years since.

Among the early names of Winston physicians we find Drs. Fries, H. Singleton Belt, J. B. Britton, G. R. Gray, King, Westmoreland, Motsinger and perhaps others for a short time. Some fifteen years ago Dr. Preston Roan located permanently in Winston and continued in active practice until his death, November 8th, 1882.

The medical fraternity as now made up in the Twin-City is a credit to the profession and we are pleased to say that they indorse what we have to say on page 5 and elsewhere regarding the healthfulness and salubrity of this section of country.

A *Physicians' Association* of Winston-Salem was organized some four years ago and is conducted in an informal manner. The place of meeting is changed each week, and matters of general interest to the profession are discussed. This, besides its social feature, has a tendency to create uniformity of action and good will between the members of the fraternity composing the organization.

DR. J. F. SHAFFNER.
PHYSICIAN AND DRUGGIST.

There is but one drug house in Salem and this, located on Main Street, contains a large and well assorted stock, kept by Dr. Schaffner, a native of the place, who graduated from the Jefferson Medical College, of Philadelphia, in 1860. A year or two later the Doctor was in the Confederate Army and in '65 began practice in Salem, shortly afterwards, purchasing his present drug stand which he has now conducted for 20 years. The house keeps drugs, paints, druggists sundries, etc., and the Doctor spends a portion of his time in practice. Dr. Shaffner has been Mayor of Salem and interested in manufacturing. In that department we made a note of his bone-mill and cotton gin which have since burned, but the Doctor informs us that he will rebuild the structure on a larger scale.

DR. H. T. BAHNSON.
OFFICE AND RESIDENCE NEAR ACADEMY

Henry T. Bahnson was born in Lancaster, Pa., brought here in childhood, graduated from the medical department of the University of Pa., in 1867, took a post graduate course in Germany and located in Salem some twenty years ago, where he has since been continuously in practice. Dr. Bahnson has long been a member of the North Carolina State Medical Society and at one time officiated as its President. He is at present a member of the State Board of Health and his long practice here has made him well known throughout the city and county.

DR. N. S. SIEWERS.
RESIDENCE NEAR PUBLIC SQUARE.

N. S. Siewers was born in Salem, graduated from the medical department of the University of Pennsylvania in 1867, going from thence to the continent where he continued his studies for a couple of years in Berlin, Prague and Vienna. He returned to Salem in 1869 and located in the town of his nativity, where he has since continued to practice his profession with good success. Dr. Siewers is a member of the State Medical Association, and has many friends in Forsyth county.

DR. J. J. HILTON.
MAIN STREET, OPP. HUNTER'S HALL.

J. J. Hilton has recently located in Salem nearly opposite Hunter's hall, and makes the fourth physician of the old town. Dr. Hilton is a native of Guilford county, graduated from the University of Maryland, and has been in practice at Hillsdale since 1882. He came to Winston in 1887 and has recently changed his office to east side of Main street Salem, below Hunter's block.

DR. R. F. GRAY.
OVER ASHCRAFT AND OWENS' STORE.

Robah F. Gray was the first male child born in Winston after the county was named, Mrs. G. L. Miller, (nee White,) having been a few days his senior. Dr. Gray graduated from the Louisville Medical College in 1877, and took a post graduate course from Bellevue College in N. Y., locating in practice here ten years since. Subsequently he spent a short time in Danville, and returned again to Winston. Dr. Gray belongs to the State Medical Societies of this State and Virginia, and for a year served Winston as Health Officer at a nominal sum. In that year small pox was brought here, and, by rigid quarantine was confined to a few cases in one part of the city. Dr. Gray is a public spirited citizen and a very active practitioner.

DR. S. J. MONTAGUE.
OFFICE ON CHURCH STREET.

S. J. Montague is a native of Wake County, attended a course of lectures at the University of Virginia, and graduated from the Bellevue Hospital Medical College in 1872. Dr. Montague practiced in his native county and elsewhere before coming to Winston in 1879, where he has since been engaged in his professional duties. He is a member of the State Medical Association. A half dozen years ago the doctor added to the architectural beauty of Church street by erecting one of the finest residences in the eastern part of the city.

DR. A. L. MOCK.
LIBERTY STREET, NEAR M. E. CHURCH.

A. L. Mock was born in Davidson County, graduated from the University of Pennsylvania in 1857, and located in Winston thirty years ago. Shortly afterwards he moved to Bethania, where he practiced for six years, and subsequently spent twenty years in practice at Clemmonsville, his native town. In 1886 Dr. Mock returned to Winston, and has his office and residence on Liberty street, near the M. E. Church. Winston has made a remarkable change since Dr. Mock's former practice here in 1858.

DR. D. N. DALTON.
OVER BROWN'S DRUG STORE.

D. N. Dalton is a native of Stokes County, and graduated from the University of N. Y. in 1881. He attended the post graduate school of N. Y., and subsequently practiced for two years in his native county before engaging in the profession here in 1884. Dr. Dalton is a member of the State Medical Association. His office is over Brown's drug store, and his residence on Spruce between 4th and 5th Streets.

DR. H. S. LOTT.
OFFICE IN GRAY BLOCK.

H. S. Lott is a native of this place, and graduated from the medical department of the University of Ga., at Atlanta, in 1884. He practiced there for a time, and locating in Winston a year since, has already gained a fair share of friends and patients. Dr. Lott has office rooms in the Gray Block and resides on Cherry street near First. He is a member of the N. C. State Medical Association.

DENTISTRY.

Dentistry is comparatively a science of modern date, and the great importance of the teeth to health, comfort and beauty, is now very much more appreciated than it was at the beginning of the present century. It is doubtless a fact, that in consequence of plain diet and rough bread, (which furnished more of the phosphates than our present system, of bolting fine flour), that the teeth of our ancestors were, as a rule, much less subject to decay than those of the present age. Be that as it may, we should make the best of what we have, and preserve the natural teeth intact as long as possible, for no artificial set can be a *perfect* substitute. The best rule for preservation, briefly given, is the rigid enforcement of absolute cleanliness. Thoroughly rinse out the mouth upon rising and retiring, and every time after eating. The quill pick, a good brush and equal quantities of prepared chalk and powdered orris root are also good adjuncts, being careful to always reach every part of each tooth. For tartar, irregularity, decay or other special conditions consult a competent dentist. Do not neglect the teeth till they ache, and always have a tooth filled if it can be saved. It is a good plan to have a dentist examine the mouth once or twice each year, as prompt treatment saves much trouble and expense.

DR. J. A. BLUM.
FOURTH STREET, WINSTON.

Is a native of this place, graduated from the Philadelphia Dental College in 1870 and has since been practicing his profession. He resides at the corner of 4th and Spruce Streets and is at present the only dentist in Winston.

DR. J. W. HUNTER.
OFFICE HUNTER BLOCK.

Born in this county, Dr. Hunter began dentistry in 1851, having now been 37 years continuously in practice, and his office shows that he keeps squarely abreast of the times in dental literature, etc. In 1874 Dr. Hunter purchased the hall and store formerly erected by Messrs. Hege, where he now holds his office. He operates for the Academy students and spends a portion of each day at that institution.

DRS. WATKINS & CONRAD.
MAIN STREET, SALEM.

C. J. Watkins was born in this county, and has been in the dental practice for 22 years. He graduated at the Pennsylvania College of Dental Surgery, practiced for several years in Philadelphia, and has been in Salem since 1874.

W. J. Conrad was also born in Forsyth, graduated from the above school in 1879, and has since operated in this county and Virginia. He joined Dr. Watkins in practice Jan. 1886. The firm keep a supply of dental goods, and both are members of the State Dental Association.

DR. H. V. HORTON.
NO. 1, CITY FLATS, SALEM.

H. V. Horton is a native of Wilkesboro, and graduated with high honors from the dental department of the University of Maryland. When he came to the Twin City he could find no suitable apartments in Winston, and finally secured an elegant suite of rooms in the City Flats of Salem. The doctor contemplates moving to Winston when the Wachovia Bank corner is completed, and as there is no dentist in the business portion of the city, and he has every requisite for successful dentistry, we think such a move would be appreciated by the progressive people of the place.

Photograph Artists
S. E. HOUGH.
Main Street, Opp. Merchants Hotel.

E. K. Hough fitted up convenient rooms for photography some years since, and a year ago sold his business to his brother, S. E. Hough, who is a native of N. Y., and has served as an artist three years in the West Indies and twelve years in New York City. The rooms are well adapted to the business, and pictures are finished up in all styles of the art. A large accumulation of negatives are on hand.

H. A. LINEBACK.
Opposite Land Office, Salem.

Salem has but one photograph gallery. H. A. Lineback is a native of Salem, and after taking instructions at several prominent galleries in Pennsylvania and Ohio, opened up the photograph business in Salem in 1866, and two years later built his present stand, where for twenty years he has turned out acceptable work. Pictures are finished in the desirable styles, and frames are carried to meet the demands of his customers.

Broker and Real Estate Agent.
H. MONTAGUE.
Broker and Real Estate Dealer.

Was born in Wake County, graduated from Wake Forest College in 1880, and after two year's course at Dick & Dillard's law school at Greensboro, was licensed to practice law in October 1882. He settled at Wadesboro where he practiced his chosen profession about two years, dealing extensively in negotiable paper and real estate in the mean time. Owing to a partial failure of vision he was compelled to abandon the practice of his profession, and in Jan. 1885 settled in Winston, having since been engaged successfully in the above occupation. He has a well arranged business house in the center of the city, and deals extensively in loans and discounts, bonds, mortgages, stocks, real estate, &c., and this mention could have properly been made under the head of banking. He handles real estate on commission, and by bringing the buyer and seller together assists in keeping up the standard values. The proprietor is not only under a justified bond of $10,000, but gives as reference the banks of Winston, and quite a number of bankers and other persons of note throughout the State.

Gun & Locksmiths.
T. VOGLER.
Gun and Locksmith.

Gun making was carried on by Vogler and Foltz at an early day, and Timothy Vogler, who was born in the place, August 2nd, 1806, began the trade with his father at 13 years of age. He has worked at his present stand near the lower end of Main street for 55 years. Mr. V. although for nearly 70 years at the gunsmith's bench, has fair health, and attends to business as occasion requires.

WM. DETTMAR.
Gunsmith, Main Street, Salem.

Is a native of Germany, learned the locksmith trade in the fatherland, came to Salem in 1850 and engaged with T. Vogler in the gunsmith business, remaining with him 18 years, when he started a shop further up town. Eight years ago Mr. D. built his present brick shop, where he does everything in the gun-smith line.

Miscellaneous Manufacturing.

[CONTINUED FROM PAGE 30.]

P. A. WILSON,
THIRD STREET.
Custom Clothier.

The description of manufacturing interests would be incomplete without a notice of clothing industries. Hon. P. A. Wilson, Sr., is a native of Rockingham County, and commenced tailoring in 1845. He has at different times been engaged in other work, but again returned to the business in 1876. He does not keep goods in stock, but has a large line of samples from which to select, and secures the cloths promptly by express from the Metropolitan cities. He gives employment to a half dozen hands, and does prompt and efficient work. Mr. Wilson has served this place as Mayor for several terms, was Deputy Internal Revenue Collector for two years, and has twice been elected a member of the Legislature.

R. D. JOHNSON,
MERCHANT TAILOR,

Fourth Street, Opposite Court House.

Robert D. Johnson is a native of this State, and after serving a long apprenticeship at the tailor's bench, took instructions in New York for a year at the cutter's trade, and was engaged in merchant tailoring at Wilson and Goldsboro for a dozen years prior to coming to this place. Mr. Johnson's experience and excellency of work soon brought to him a large trade, and in 1880 he erected his fine three story brick building on Fourth Street, opposite the Court house. The upstairs is used for secret societies, the second story for offices and the lower floor for the merchant tailoring business. Ten to twelve hands are given employment and a large amount of work turned out. Customers who once secure perfect fits and good workmanship do not soon forget the place, and Mr. J. sends his goods to many distant States. A large stock of foreign and domestic cloths are kept on hand, and the class of work done is a credit to the proprietor and the place.

G. A. REICH.
Boot and Shoe Maker.

G. Adolphus Reich, is a Salemite by birth, and nearly 40 years ago began his trade at the shoe-maker's bench and continued in the trade till the war. Later he operated as cutter for prominent firms in this State, and also in Philadelphia. In 1875 he engaged with his brother as a partner in the firm of H. C. Reich & Co., and five years later, on the dissolution of that firm, moved his headquarters to his present location near the lower end of Main street, in Salem. Mr. Reich is a good judge of leather, a good workman, and has many customers that have been using his work for a dozen years or more.

IRVING BLUM,
Grocer, Tin and Coppersmith.

On the old Blum homestead, near the north end of Winston, is found the tin and copper works of Irving Blum, who was raised in this line of trade, and has copper work sent for repairs, to his shop, from long distances. A year ago Mr. Blum started a grocery business near by, and keeps a line of fancy and plain articles in that department of trade.

Wm. H. Hall began candy making in Salem 35 years ago, and excepting a few months during the war has been at it continuously since. He is now turning his attention largely to bees, having over 90 stands in his apiary.

The Salem Grist Mill commenced business in 1825, and continues to grind both corn and wheat under the proprietorship of C. P. Sides.

[CONTINUED ON PAGE 65.]

WINSTON'S GRADED SCHOOL BUILDING—See Page 15.

AN EPITOME OF
VALUABLE STATISTICS
AND
GENERAL INFORMATION.

INTRODUCTORY.

In order to make this pamphlet of value to every person who receives it, we incorporate in this department many facts and dates which have required great labor and expense to prepare. These dates are so valuable that no one can afford to destroy them and hence the book will be preserved with absolute certainty whether the remaining pages are of interest to the reader or not. This book will be convenient for reference and containing so many interesting facts and dates will be preserved in the library for months and years, thus making it worth from a business standpoint, a circulation of twenty times as great a number of newspapers.

THE WORLD IN A NUT SHELL.

CHRONOLOGICAL DATES.

The history of the world up to the time of the deluge and for many years afterwards is only to be found in the brief narrative given in the sacred writings, although the Chinese claim to have records dating back to a period long before "Adam was born."

THE HEBREWS.

Deluge B. C. 2350; Abraham called 1921; Joseph in Egypt, 1725; Birth of Moses, 1571; Hebrews left Egypt, 1491; death of Moses, 1451; Deborah Judge of Israel, 1385; Gideon slaughtered Midianites 1245; Jeptha, Judge, 1288; Eli, Judge, 1256; Sampson, 1237; Samuel, 1229; Saul King, 1195; David King, 1155; Solomon King, 1115; Temple dedicated 1104; Solomon died 1075; division of Israel 1056; Elijah and Elisha prophets, 888; Jerusalem taken by Jehoash 826; Hezekiah and Isaiah in Judah 726; Jeremiah prophet 641; Jerusalem taken by Nebuchadnezzar, 606; Jerusalem destroyed, 588.

EGYPT.

Little or nothing is known of the history of Egypt prior to the time of Joseph. At that time however it was one of the most powerful nations of the world. The dynasty of the Pharaohs, B. C., 1900; Pyramids built by Cheops, 1082; Shishak ruler, 978; Judea conquered and the temple plundered by him 971; Egypt devastated by Nebuchadnezzar, 572; end of the first Egyptian monarchy 525 and for over 200 years it was in obscurity, but revived again by the Ptolemys about three centuries before Christ. Cleopatra lived B. C. 45 and Egypt was again subdued B. C. 30.

MACEDON.

was subdued by Darius, B. C. 508; Philip II crowned 359; Alexander in Macedon 336; invaded Persia 334; battle of Arabela 331; Alexander died at Babylon of strong drink, aged 32, B. C. 324.

GREECE.

By valor and refinement, Greece became the next nation in importance. Troy was taken B. C. 1184. Ionians settled in Asia 1043; Homer the poet, wrote about 888; first Olympiad period from which the Greeks reckon time, 776; Code of Draco 621; Solon, Athenian law-giver 594; Socrates 429; war with Macedon 358; Republic re-established 297; Corinth taken 146.

ROME.

founded by Romulus 753; Tarquin the elder, 616; Tarquin the proud, 534; Brutus 509; Cincinnatus dictator 456; great famine 440; invaded by the Gauls 391; first Punic war 265; second Punic war 218; third war 149; Carthage destroyed 146; Cicero 63; Cesar invades Britian 55; dictator 45; Cesar assassinated 41; Augustus emperor, 30. CHRISTIAN ERA. The bloody Nero A. D. 54; Jerusalem destroyed by Titus 70 rebuilt 147; Persian war 231; persecution of Christians 236; Constantine emperor 323; Council at Nice, when the books of the New Testament were voted in, 325; Romans driven from Spain 469; withdrew from Britian 419; battle of Chalons 451; Odoacer king of Itauli; puts an end to the Roman empire.

MEDES & PERSIANS.

Darius, king B. C. 521; second Temple dedicated 515; Darius invades Greece 494; Artaxerxes I 464; Esther queen 478; Nehemiah rebuilds Jerusalem 455; conquered and claimed by the macedons 335.

EASTERN EMPIRE, ETC.

A. D. 447. Attila king of Huns exacts tribute from Theodosius II; ravaged by Persians 503; Jostlinian code 529; Mohammed preaching 612; Persians take Syria 614; the Hegira 622; Saracens besiege Constantinople 673-7; their second siege of Constantinople 718; Michael II 820; John Zimisces 969; Turks take Jerusalem 1065; Crusaders take Antioch 1098, and Jerusalem 1099, and Acre 1104; Venice in her glory 1125; Latin conquers 1204; Empire recovered by Greeks 1261; Turkish Empire Osman I, 1298; Suppression of Knights Templar 1311; general pestilence 1348; Empire excepting Constantinople taken by the Turks 1381; Union of Denmark, Sweeden and Norway 1307; invention of printing 1438; Constantinople captured by Turks and end of Empire 1453; Ferdinand and Isabela in Spain 1479; Columbus discovered America 1492.

FRANCE.

Clovis makes Paris his capital A. D. 507; Clovis II king of France 656; Cadwallader last king of Britons 678; Charles Martel duke of France 710; battle of

Tours 732; Danes in England 787; Charlemagne emporer of the west 800; Charles the Bald in France 814; Rollo the Norman 912; Hugh Capet 987; Henry I 1031; Philip I 1060; first crusade 1096; war with England 1098; Louis the Fat 1108; Louis VII 1137; Philip II 1180; Louis IX (St. Louis) 1226; Louis X 1314; House of Valois 1328; Charles V 1364; Joan of Arc enters Orleans 1428; France ridden of English 1451; French take Milan 1494; Huguenot war 1562; massacre of St. Bartholomew 1572; House of Bourbon 1589; Cardinal Richelieu 1624; invasion of Holland 1672; Louis XV 1715; France aids America 1778; revolution 1790; republic 1792; Napoleon consul 1793; Emperor 1804; campaign in Russia 1812; fall of Napoleon 1815; conquest of Algiers 1837; Louis Napoleon president, 1848; Napoleon III emperor 1852; French in Mexico 1863; war with Prussia 1870; Republic; Thiers president, 1871 Jules Grevy president 1879; occupation of Anam and trouble with China 1884.

ITALY AND COTEMPORARY.

Lombards take Italy A. D. 536; defeat Constans II 662; and conquered by Charlemagne 774; the Crusades 1099 to 1538; wars of Charles V in Italy 1527; capture of Rome 1527; order of Jesuits founded 1555; calendar remodeled by pope Gregory XII 1582; Peter Great in Russia 1689; Frederick II in Prussia 1740; French in Spain 1808; Moscow burned 1812; Greece independent 1827; siege of Sebastopol 1854; Victor Emanuel King of Italy 1861; revolution in Spain 1868; Russia-Turkish war 1877; Humbert King of Italy 1879; assassination of Alexander II of Russia 1881; Alexander III crowned 1883.

GERMANY.

House of France 814; Henry I defeats the danes 934; war with the Saracens 1073; Frederick I invades Italy 1154; destroys Milan 1162; House of Hapsburg 1273; revolt of Swiss and Wm. Tell 1307; House of Luxemberg 1349; John Huss burned by Sigismund 1415; House of Austria 1438; Maximilian I 1493; reformation by Luther 1517; Maximilian II 1564; battle of Prague 1620; Leopold I 1659; House of Lorraine 1745.

PRUSSIA.

Takes Hanover 1801; war with France 1813; German Confederation 1815; war with Denmark 1864, and Austria 1866, invasion of France 1870, William made emperor 1871 and died 1888, succeeded by Frederick March 13 1888.

AUSTRIA.

An empire 1800, war with France 1813, with Hungary 1848, with France and Italy 1859, withdrawal from the confederation 1870, international exhibition at Vienna 1873, agreement with Germany on Eastern question 1880.

ENGLAND.

Anglo Saxon Kings 825, Egbert 828, Alfred the great 871, ravages of Scotland 933, Danish Kings 1016, Saxons restored 1041, English language originates from the Saxon, Danish, British, Welsh, Norman, Latin, French and Greek A. D. 1000 to 1500, Norman Dynasty 1066, conquest of Ireland 1171, conquest of Wales 1282, battle of Bannockburn 1314, House of Lancaster 1399, war with France 1415, House of York 1461, House of Tudor 1485, battle of Flodden 1513, Ann Boleyn beheaded 1536 and Mary of Scots 1587, House of Stuart 1603, Oliver Cromwell 1649, Stuarts restored 1659, great London fire 1666, battle of the Boyne 1690 House of Hanover 1714, war with Spain 1739, with France 1756, war with colonies 1775, Union with Ireland 1801, war with U. S. 1812, battle of Waterloo 1815, Victoria crowned queen 1837, Crimean war 1854, Atlantic cable laid 1866, Fenian trouble 1867, Zulu war 1879, famine in Ireland 1880, war with Egypt 1882, Gladstone's bill or relief of Ireland 1887.

AMERICA, OUR HOME.

Discovered by Norsemen A D 980, Iceland settled 985, Lief visited Newfoundland and Massachusetts 1001, discovered by Columbus 1492, Florida entered by Ponce de Leon 1512, Balboa discovers the Pacific 1513, Cortez in Mexico 1519, Pizarro in Peru 1532, Desoto in Florida and Louisiana 1541, St. Augustine founded 1565 Jamestown, Va., 1607, Quebec 1608, New York 1614, Plymouth Rock 1620, Swedes in Delaware 1627, Maryland settled 1634, Connecticut 1635, New Jersey and North Carolina 1664, South Carolina 1674, Pennsylvania 1682, Georgia by Oglethorpe 1733, New Hampshire 1741, Quebec taken 1759, Canada ceeded to England by the French '61, Revolutionary war '75 Declaration of Independence July 4th, '776, surrender of Cornwallis '81, treaty of peace '83, constitution adopted '87, Washington made president, '89, Louisiana ceeded to U. S. 1803, war with England 1812, Florida ceeded '20, Buenos Ayres independent '16, Mexico '21, Texas '35, annexed '45, war with Mexico '46, civil war '61, Maximilian emperor '64, U. S. buys Alaska '67, war in Cuba '71, Chili-Peru war '81, Mexico building railroad '82.

ADDITION OF STATES.

Vermont admitted 1791, Kentucky 1792, Tennessee 1796, Ohio 1802, Louisiana admitted '12, Indiana admitted '16, Mississippi '17 Illinois '18, Alabama '19, Maine '20, Missouri '21, Arkansas '36, Michigan '37, Texas annexed '45, Florida admitted '45, Iowa '46, New Mexico and California purchased '48, Wisconsin admitted '48, California '50, Minnesota '58, Oregon '59, Kansas '61, West Virginia '63, Nevada '64, Nebraska '67, Southern States re-admitted '68, Colorado '76. With the exception of the years 1821 to '36 the United States has never before in her history of a century been so long without admitting a new State. Dakota, Wyoming and Utah are knocking for admission and with some legal technicalities removed will probably soon be within the fold.

INTERNAL AND FOREIGN.

Wayne's victory at Maumee 1794, Jay's treaty '95, with France '97, Government removed from Philadelphia to Washington, D. C., '99, trial of Aaron Burr for Conspiracy 1807, Perry's victory Sept. 10, '13, Washington burned '14, battle of New Orleans '15, Missouri compromise '20, Lafayette's visit '21, John Adams and Thomas Jefferson, 2d and third presidents died July 4 '26, protective tariff bill passed '28, treaty with Turkey '30, Blackhawk war '32, Seminole war '35, financial crisis '37, veto of bank bill '41, gold in California '48, Taylor died July 9th, '50, Kansas trouble '55, treaty with Japan '54, Mormon insurrection, Dred-Scot decision '57, John Brown's insurrection '59, South Carolina seceded Dec. 20 '60, Miss., Ala., Fla., Ga., La., Tx., Va., Ark., Tenn. and North Carolina follow and Jefferson Davis elected president of the Southern Confederacy '61, bombardment of Fort Sumter and battle of Bull Run '61, Antietam, Ft. Donaldson, Pea Ridge, Shiloh, 2d Bull Run, Corinth, Fredericksburg, '62. Emancipation Proclamation Jan. 1, '63, battles of Chancellorville, Vicksburg, Gettysburg, '63, Wilderness, Petersburg and Sherman's March to the Sea, '64, battle of Five Forks, surrender of Lee, Johnson and Kirby Smith and end of war '65, impeachment and acquittal of President Johnson '68, Fifteenth Amendment '70, great fire in Chicago '71, Modoc war '73, Custer massacre and Centennial Exposition '76, great railroad riots '77, resumption of specie payment '79, treaty with China '81, general strike of telegraph operators '83, World's Exposition New Orleans '84-5, great flood of the Ohio Feb. '85, earthquake at Charleston, '86, great railroad disaster at Chatsworth, Illinois, over 100 persons killed '87. Ex-Senator Conkling and Chief Justice Waite died '88.

GENERAL INFORMATION

CANADA, OUR NORTHERN NEIGHBOR.

The government of Canada is subject to the British crown but is semi-independent, its history dating back to the sixteenth century. Jacques Cartier, a French sea captain planted his standard on the shores of New Brunswick in 1534 and claimed it for France. Later he discovered the river St. Lawrence. General Wolfe's forces captured Quebec in 1759 and the entire country was claimed for the British. During the Revolutionary struggle for independence the Canadian settlements remained true to the king and after and during the war many exiles fled from the colonies to Upper Canada, now called Ontario, while the eastern province is known as Quebec, or Lower Canada.

Canada proper covers 375,000 square miles and has a population of about 4,750,000 inhabitants while the remainder of the Brittish Possessions in North America covers an area ten times as great and has only about one-third as many inhabitants. In 1825 Ontario had a population of 158,027; '52, 952,004 and in '86 about two millions. The Canadian Pacific railroad now more than half completed, will open to settlement an immense tract of country and be the fourth iron highway across the continent. The Central Pacific completed in 1868 having made the first through connection from the Atlantic to the Pacific ocean. Canada proper is the most fertile and salubrious of the British American territory; even the frigid regions of the Northwest Territory and Manitoba are gaining in population. Winnipeg the capital city of the latter country is rapidly rising to prominence. The summer seasons although short are warm and the growth of vegetation marvelous.

MEXICO, OUR SOUTHERN BORDER.

The history of Mexico up to the time of its conquest by Cortez is almost unknown. When De Cordova discovered the country in 1517 he found the Aztecs Nation in possession of the land. These people were far in advance of the aboriginals who occupied the territory now belonging to the U. S. They had a monarchial government, cities and agricultural lands, were versed in astronomy and the working of metals, pottery, etc., yet had nothing but tradition as to their ancestry or origin. Some writers consider them of the highest type of Indian civilization while others believe them to have descended from a different source. Their habits and manners make it reasonable to infer that they were contemporaries with, and perhaps the same race as the Moundbuilders of the Ohio Valley, whose tumuli still remain as monuments to their skill and devotion. Montezuma was monarch of the Aztecs when the country was taken by Fernando Cortez 1519-21 and thenceforth for nearly 300 years Mexico was under Spanish rule. The revolution of 1810 by the natives was a most bloody scene and resulted in the destruction of thousands of lives. Don Augustin Iturbide a native Mexican Spaniard ten years later led a successful revolt and the independence of Mexico was established in 1821. Since then the government has had numerous changes but is at present essentially like the U. S. in form.

Mexico covers an area of 741,589 square miles and has a population of about ten millions of inhabitants. Its table lands are salubrious and fertile and with two through railroad lines from Texas, this easy going republic will doubtless fall into the rapid march of enterprise and refinement.

CUBA, OUR ISLAND NEIGHBOR.

The greatest of Spain's colonial possessions was discovered by Columbus in 1492, and in 1511 Velasquez conquered the natives. Havana was founded 1519. Cuba has been more prosperous since the advent of Las Cassas as governor-general in 1790 but has had numerous bickerings and revolts. A serious revolt occurred in 1868, which caused the sacrifice of 56,000 Cuban soldiers and cost the Spanish government more than twenty millions of dollars to quell. It is still tributary to Spain but groans under the yoke and longs for annexation to the U. S. from which it is separated by less than 100 miles of ocean.

The limit of these pages will not permit of giving detailed facts regarding Central and South America, but our relations with the mother country are so intimate that we shall appropriate some space to her consideration next.

GREAT BRITAIN, OUR MOTHER COUNTRY.

The history of Great Britain properly commences with the conquests of Cæsar B C 55. The Roman rule lasted till 420 A D. The Scots, Huns, Danes and other tribes ravaged the country and internal dissensions continued until the establishment of the Norman line A D 1066. The first parliament was convened in 1265 and thirty years later a session of commons was added, these being a concession wrung from the Kings by the Barons. King Charles attempted to dispense with parliament, but was overthrown by Oliver Cromwell in 1645. The Habeas Corpus Act was passed in 1679 on the return of the Stuarts to the throne. The government is a constitutional monarchy, the executive power being vested in the sovereign and the legislative in parliament. The area of Great Britain including Ireland covers 121,377 square miles and has about 36,000,000 people. The entire British Possession covers an area of 7,788,347 square miles and having a population of over 300,000,000 inhabitants, or about one-fourth of humanity. Other European countries deserve a separate mention but we must refer the reader to more extensive history.

EIGHTEEN DECISIVE BATTLES
In the World's History.

Marathon by Miltaocles B C 490, Athenians—Persians.

Syracuse by Glippus B C 414, Syracusans—Spartans.

Arbela by Alexander B C 331, Greeks—Persians.

Metaurus by Nero, B C 207, Romans—Carthaginians.

Winfeldlippe by Arminius A D 9, Germans—Romans.

Chalons by Actius, 451, Romans, etc—Hunns.

Tours by Charles Martel, 732, Franks—Saracens.

Hastings by William, 1066, Normans—Anglo-Saxons.

Orleans by Joan of Arc, 1429, French—English.

Armada by Effingham, 1588, English and Dutch—Spaniards.

Blenheim by Marlborough, 1704, English and Aust. French and Bavarians.

Pultowa by Peter Great 1709, Russia—Sweeden.

Saratoga by Gates, 1777, Americans—English.

Waterloo by Wellington and Blucher 1815, English and Prussian—French.

Sedan '70, Prussians—French.

Selastopol '54-5, Eng. French Turks—Russia.

Gettysburg by Meade, '63, Union—Confederacy.

☞ Names of places appear first, prominent general next, date, victorious army, defeated forces last.

Population and Debt of Cities of the United States.

Name of Place.	Population Census 1880.	Debt 1889.	For each person.
Akron Ohio	16,511	$ 17,649	$ 1.06
Albany New York	90,903	7,138,000	81.62
Alleghany Penn'yl'na	78,684	1,206,420	20.29
Allentown do	18,063	539,443	23.83
Alexandria Virginia	13,658	1,037,668	77.32
Altoona Pennsylvana	19,716	508,820	18.70
Atchison Kansas	15,106	440,687	29.26
Atlanta Georgia	31,389	2,150,000	68.38
Auburn New York	22,924	329,060	17.32
Augusta Georgia	23,021	1,361,319	18.58

Valuable Statistics

Austin Texas	10,960	196,744	9 73
Baltimore Maryland	332,190	27,022,690	81 55
Bangor Maine	16,827	2,661,000	158 15
Bay City Michigan	20,693	422,100	20 56
Binghamton New York	17,315	309,544	17 29
Bloomington Illinois	17,184	221,463	12 88
Boston Massachusetts	362,535	28,244,017	77 80
Bridgeport Connecticut	29,145	811,040	28 51
Brooklyn New York	566,689	38,040,080	67 13
Buffalo New York	155,137	8,211,604	52 93
Burlington Iowa	19,450	128,082	6 58
Cambridge Mass	52,749	3,365,523	64 33
Camden New Jersey	41,658	1,164,060	27 96
Charleston S Carolina	29,9.9	1,129,102	82 58
Chattanooga Tennessee	12,892	71,596	5 55
Davenport Iowa	21,834	299,675	13 31
Evansville Indiana	29,280	none	
Erie Pennsylvania	27,730	1,204,229	43 34
Elmyra New York	20,541	270,400	13 17
East Saginaw Mich	19,016	611,055	32 13
Fall River Mass	49,006	3,169,765	64 68
Grand Rapids Mich	32,015	471,060	14 71
Galveston Texas	22,254	1,023,249	45 97
Hoboken New Jersey	30,969	1,009,229	33 16
Houston Texas	18,646	1,504,791	80 53
Indianapolis Indiana	75,074	1,914,744	25 50
Kansas City Missouri	55,813	1,339,224	23 99
Louisville Kentucky	123,645	4,842,985	39 16
Lewiston Maine	19,083	1,038,102	54 39
Milwaukee Wisconsin	115,578	2,160,228	18 69
Minneapolis Minn	36,887	1,152,467	21 25
Memphis Tennessee	33,586	none	
Manchester N H	32,630	929,000	28 19
Mobile Alabama	31,385	2,671,100	85 91
New York N Y	1,206,590	109,425,414	90 69
New Orleans Louisiana	216,140		
Norfolk Virginia	21,966	2,187,571	99 57
Newport Kentucky	20,433	905,618	42 41
Nashville Tennessee	43,461	1,006,290	26 95
Oakland California	34,556	662,126	19 55
Omaha Nebraska	30,518	227,578	7 45
Oswego New York	21,117	1,264,224	59 86
Oshkosh Wisconsin	15,749	450,564	8 28
Pittsburg Pennsylvania	156,384	11,134,286	70 37
Providence Rhode Is	104,850		
Patterson New Jersey	50,887	1,370,590	26 71
Portland Maine	33,840	4,332,151	128 13
Peoria Illinois	29,315	716,560	24 44
Petersburg Virginia	21,656	1,126,160	52 46
Poughkeepsie N Y	20,207	1,809,158	85 46

Presidents, Vice-Presidents and Public Debts.

Presidents, Vice-Presidents, and a statement of the Public Debt, including accrued interest thereon less cash in the Treasury on the 1st day of July, of each, year compiled from the published Report of the Secretary of the Treasury.

Year	President	Vice-President	Debt
1789	Washington	Adams	
1793	Washington	Adams	$80,352,634 04
1797	Adams	Jefferson	$82,064,479 33
1801	Jefferson	Burr	$3,038,050 80
1805	Jefferson	Clinton	$2,312,150 50
1809	Madison	Clinton	57,023,192 09
1813	Madison	Gerry	55,962,827 57
1817	Monroe	Tompkins	123,491,965 16
1821	Monroe	Tompkins	89,987,427 66
1825	J.Q. Adams	Calhoun	83,788,432 71
1829	Jackson	Calhoun	58,421,413 67
1833	Jackson	Van Buren	7,001,698 83
1837	Van Buren	Johnson	336,957 83
1841	Harrison	Tyler	5,250,875 54
1842	Tyler	Wm. P. Mangum	13,594,480 73
1845	Polk	Dallas	15,925,303 01
1849	Taylor	Fillmore	63,061,858 69
1850	Fillmore	King	63,452,773 55
1853	Pierce	King	59,881,117 70
1857	Buchanan	Breckenridge	28,699,831 85
1861	Lincoln	Hamlin	90,580,873 72
1865	Lincoln	Johnson	2,680,647,869 74
1866	Johnson	Foster	2,773,236,173 69
1869	Grant	Colfax	2,489,002,480 58
1873	Grant	Wilson	2,147,818,713 57
1877	Hayes	Wheeler	2,060,158,223 26
1881	Garfield	Arthur	1,840,598,811 98
1882	Arthur	Davis	1,688,914,460 72
1886	Cleveland	Hendricks	1,417,156,362 00

Brief Biography of Presidents.

George Washington, born Va. 1782, died '99, Aid-de-camp to Braddock Indian campaign '55, chosen to Colonial Congress '74, Commander-in-chief '75, president '89-97.

John Adams, born Mass. 1735, died 1826, first vice-president and 2d president U.S., defeated by Jefferson in 1800, one of the founders of the Republic.

Thomas Jefferson, of Va. 1743, died 1826, in Colonial Congress 1775, drafted Declaration of Independence '76, governor of Va., '79, minister at Paris '85, Sec. of State '89, vice-president '96, president 1801-9.

James Madison of Va. born 1751, died 1836, one of the founders of the Federal party. Elected congress '89, sec. of State 1840, president 1809-17.

James Monroe, of Va. 1758, 1831, elected to congress 1783, governor of Va. 1799, Envoy to France 1802, secretary of state '11, president '17-'25.

John Quincy Adams, of Mass., 1767, 1848, president '25-'29, defeated by Jackson '28, elected to congress '30. His oratory gained for him the title of "Old Man Eloquent."

Andrew Jackson, of S. C. 1767, 1845, was rather illiterate, in congress 1796, U. S. senate 1797, distinguished at the battle of New Orleans, president '15, '29-37.

Martin VanBuren, of N. Y. 1782, 1862, elected state senator N. Y. 1808, state attorney-general '15, U. S. senator '21; governor '28, secretary of state '19, '29, vice-president '33, president '37-'41.

William H. Harrison, of Va. 1773, 1841, aid-de-camp to Gen. Wayne in Indian war, territorial governor of Indiana 1801-'13, defeated Indians at Tippecanoe '11, elected to congress '16, senator '24, elected president '40, and died one month after his inauguration.

John Tyler, of Va. 1790, 1862, elected to congress 1816, governor of Va. '25, U. S. senator '27, vice-president under Harrison and succeeded him April 4th '41.

James K. Polk, of N. C. 1795, 1849, congressman from Tenn. '25, governor '39, president '45 to '49. During his term Texas was annexed and the war with Mexico prosecuted.

Zachary Taylor, of Va. 1784, 1850, served in Seminole and Blackhawk war, major-general in Mexican war and won the battles of Resaca and Buena Vista, inaugurated president '49 and died July 9th 1850.

Millard Fillmore, of N. Y. 1808, 1874, congress '32, elected vice-president '48 and succeeded to the presidency on the death of Taylor.

Franklin Pierce, of N. H. 1804, 1869, congress '32, senator '37, brigadier-general in Mexican war, elected president '52, opposed coercion of the south '61.

James Buchanan, of Pa. 1791, 1868, congress '21, minister to Russia '32, U. S. senator '34, secretary of state '45, minister to England '53, president '57.

Abraham Lincoln, of Ky. 1809, elected to Ill. legislature '34, congress '46, defeated by Douglass for U. S. senator '54, elected president '60, re-elected '64 and assassinated April 14 '65 by John Wilkes Booth.

Andrew Johnson, N. C. 1808, 1875, congress from Tenn. '43, governor '53, U. S. senator '57, military governor '62, elected vice-president '64, and succeeded to the presidency on the assassination of Lincoln. He was subsequently elected U. S. senator.

Ulysses S. Grant, of Ohio, 1822, 1885, served in

Mexico, colonel of 21st Ill. vols. and brigadier-general '62, commander-in-chief '64, president '69-77.

Rutherford B. Hayes, of Conn. 1822, brigadier-general from Ohio, congress '65, question as to validity of electoral votes decided by special commission 8 to 7 and Hayes inaugurated '77.

James A. Garfield, of Ohio, 1831, professor of Latin and Greek at Hiram college and chosen president of that institution '58, state senate '59, col. '61, brigadier '62, congress '62, U. S. senator '80, president '81, shot by Giteau July 2, '81, died Sept. 19th.

Chester A. Arthur, of Vt. 1831, 1886, N. Y. lawyer, collector of port of N. Y., '71, elected vice-president '80 and succeeded to the presidency on the death of Garfield.

Grover Cleveland, of N. J., 1837, teacher in N. Y. Blind Asylum, lawyer in Buffalo, sheriff '80, mayor '81, elected governor of N. Y. by 192,000 majority '81, president '84, re-nominated '88.

Prominent Personages.

Joseph Addison, 1672, 1719, English poet and moralist, author of "The Campaign," under secretary of state 1705.

Thomas B. Aldrich, 1836, Am. poet and novelist, Prudence Palfry, etc.

Ethan Allen, 1742, '89, commander in Revolutionary war, hero of Ticonderoga and Crown Point.

Benedict Arnold, 1740, 1801, American general and traitor, later colonel in British army.

John Jacob Astor, of Heidelberg, Germany, 1763, 1848, rose rapidly to wealth in N. Y. merchandise. Founded the Astor Library.

Francis Bacon, 1561, 1626, English statesman, jurist and philosopher. Queen's counsel at age of 28, solicitor-general 1607.

Sir Samuel Baker, 1821, English African explorer author geographical and literary works.

Nathaniel P. Banks, 1816, American general and politician, congress '52, governor of Mass. 3 terms.

Benj. D. Beaconsfield, 1804, 1880, English statesman and novelist, chancellor of exchequer, prime minister '68.

P. T. G. Beauregard, 1816, confederate general at Ft. Sumter, Bull Run and Shiloh.

Thos. H. Benton, 1782, 1858, of Hillsboro, N. C. Elected to U. S. senate from Mo. 1820, and congress '52.

James G. Blaine, of Pa. 1830, congress from Maine '62, U. S. senator '77, secretary under Garfield, candidate for presidency '84.

Daniel Boone, of Pa. 1735, 1820, pioneer Ky., Ind., Ill. and Missouri. Prominent Indian fighter.

John C. Breckenridge, of Ky. 1821, 1875, vice-president under Buchanan, candidate for president '60, U. S. Senator '61, resigned and entered confederate service as general and later secretary of war for the confederacy.

John Brown, of Conn. 1800, zealous abolitionist, headed negro insurrection at Harper's Ferry '59 and was hanged by Gov. Wise, of Va. the same year.

Robt. Burns, 1759, 1796, Scotchman and author of many prominent poems.

Aaron Burr, 1756, 1836, lawyer and statesman, vice-president under Jefferson, killed Hamilton in duel, was tried for treason but acquitted.

Benj. F. Butler, of N. H., 1818, lawyer, politician and general, military governor of New Orleans, '62, congress from Mass. '66, governor '82.

Lord Byron, 1788, 1824, English poet, espoused the cause of Greek liberty and died in Greece.

Thos. Carlyle, 1795, 1881, Scotch essayist, biographer, historian and mathematician.

Marcus T. Cicero, B. C. 106, '43, Roman author, statesman orator, exiled B. C. 58, but recalled. Killed by Antony's soldiers.

Henry Clay, of Va. 1777, 1852, statesman and orator, U. S. senate 1806, signed treaty of Ghent '15, candidate for president '32 and '44, prominently connected with the compromise of 1830.

Saml. T. Coleridge, 1772, 1834, English poet and critic, German linguist and wrote Lyrical Ballads.

Christopher Columbus, of Genoa, Italy, 1436, 1506, sailed from Palos Aug. 3, 1492, reached San Salvador Oct. 12 of that year and gave the natives the name of Indians, discovered Jamaica and Porto Rico 1495, and South America 1498.

Confucius, B. C. 551, 478, Chinese philosopher, commenced preaching at 22, originated the "Golden Rule" and taught that to be polite and do good to humanity should be the chief end of man. Two-thirds of the human race for 2,300 years have given great credence to the precepts which he enunciated.

Copernicus, 1473, 1543, German astronomer, disproved the Ptolemaic theory and demonstrated that the sun is the center of the universe.

Wm. Cowper, 1731, 1800, English poet, translated Homer 1784. His letters and poetry are highly eulogized.

Charles R. Darwin, 1809, '82, English naturalist and originated the theory of "evolution," that all forms of animal or vegetable life progress in the scale of natural descent by the "survival of the fittest."

Jefferson Davis, of Ky., 1808, U. S. senator from Miss., '47, inaugurated president of the Confederacy '61, imprisoned in Fortress Monroe for 2 years after the fall of Richmond, released on bail with Horace Greeley and other northern men as sureties and later the indictment quashed.

Daniel Defoe, 1661, 1731, English novelist, in insurrection against James II. Author of over 200 works.

John B. DeKalb, 1732, 1780, German general, accompanied Lafayette to Am. 1777 and killed at battle of Camden S. C. '80.

Demosthenes, B. C. 385, 322, Athenian orator, opposed Philip of Macedon against whom he delivered his "Phillippics." Oration on the crown his greatest achievement. Suicided by poison.

Charles Dickens, 1812, '70, English novelist, for a time reporter for the press, author of Nicholas Nickolby, David Copperfield, Oliver Twist and other prominent productions.

Stephen A. Douglas, of Vt., 1817, '61, statesman, congress from Illinois, '43, senator '47, candidate for presidency '56, '60. Supported Federal war, '61.

Frederick Douglas, of Md., 1817, greatest colored American orator. Sold to a shipbuilder '32, escaped to Mass. and assumed the name of Douglas. Employed as orator for the American Anti-slavery Society '41.

Dryden, 1631, 1700, English poet, critic and dramatist, wrote "Ode on Alexander's Feast."

Mme. Dudevant, 1804, '76, French novelist, married at 18, 10 years later separated, changed from zealous catholic to liberalist, adopting man's attire and denouncing the marriage system.

Thomas A. Edison, 1847, Am. electrician and inventor of improved telegraphy, telephone, electric light, phonograph, etc.

Geo. F. Edmunds, of Vt. 1828, U. S. senator '66, re-elected three terms, and president of the senate under Arthur and after the death of Hendricks.

Ralph W. Emerson, of Mass. 1803, '82, essayist,

philosopher and poet, Unitarian minister '29, author of "Representative Men."

Edward Everett, 1794, 1865, orator and statesman, Prof. of Greek at Harvard '35; congress '24, governor of Mass. '35, minister to England '41, secretary of state '52, senate '53,.

Henry Fielding, 1707, 1754, English novelist and dramatist, lieutenant-general, "Tom Jones" his greatest novel.

Benj. Franklin, of Mass. 1706, 1790, statesman and philosopher, youngest of 17 children, printer, established Penna. Gazette, published "Poor Richard's Almanac" 1755, drew electricity from the clouds by a kite '52, minister to France '76, governor of Penn. '85, member of constitutional convention '87.

Robert Fulton, of Penn'a, 1765, 1815, engineer and inventor of steam boat, invented submarine torpedo in Paris, discovered steam navigation 1801, assisted by Robert Livingston, built steamer Clermont 1806, which ran regularly between New York and Albany.

Galileo, 1564, 1642, Italian astronomer, adopted copernican theory and constructed telescope 1609, discovered Jupiter's moons and ascertained that the "Milky Way" was composed of myriads of stars.

Edward Gibbon, 1737, 1794, English historian, author of the "Decline and Fall of the Roman Empire." He was liberal in his religious belief.

Oliver Goldsmith, 1728, '74, Irish poet and author of several prominent novels.

Jay Gould, of Sandusky, Ohio, 1836, has become prominent as a railway and telegraph owner and manager.

Horace Greeley, of N. H. 1811, 1872, journalist, founded N. Y. Tribune '41, was democratic candidate for president '72, defeated by Grant and died shortly afterwards.

Gutenberg, 1400, 1468, German inventor of printing and first publisher of the bible.

Alex. Hamilton, born in West Indies 1757; killed in duel by Aaron Burr, 1804, orator, statesman and general in revolutionary war.

Wade Hampton, of S. C. 1818, Confederate general, governor of S. C. 1876, U. S. senator '78.

Winfield S. Hancock, 1824, 1886, major-general in late war, prominent in Gettysburg fight, democratic candidate for presidency 1880.

Hannibal, B. C. 247, 183, Carthaginian general, subdued the Spaniards, captured Saguntum 219, routed Roman army 216, defeated by Scipio Africanus, 202, suicided by poison to escape being prisoner of the Romans.

Francis Bret Harte, of N. Y. 1839, humoristic writer; consul to a German port, '78, author of "Heathen Chinee," etc.

Warren Hastings, 1732, 1818, British general and statesman, governor-general of India, defeated Hyder Ali, king of Mysore.

Nathaniel Hawthorne, 1804, 1864, Am. author, Twice told tales, Scarlet Letter, Blithedale Romances, etc.

Robert Y. Hayne, 1791, 1840, Am. orator and statesman, opponent of Webster in discussion of constitution, governor of S. C. 1832.

Patrick Henry, 1736, 1799, Am. patriot and orator, in continental congress, governor of Virginia.

Oliver Wendell Holmes, 1809, Am. physician, author and poet. The Autocrat of the Breakfast Table, Elsie Venner, etc.

Homer, B. C. 1000, Greek poet, regarded as one of the greatest. Supposed to have been blind and poor. The Iliad and Odyssey are prominent text books.

Horace, B. C. '65, Latin poet, Odes, Epistles and Satires.

Samuel Houston, 1793, 1863, Am. general and statesman, governor of Tennessee '27, commander of Texas forces in revolt against Mexico, captured Santa Anna '36, and elected president of Texas, U. S. senator and governor of Texas.

Washington Irving, of New York, 1783, 1859, author Knickerbocker's History of N. Y. secretary of legation at London '29, minister to Spain '42, "Bracebridge Hall," "Conquest of Grenada," etc. are among his works.

Stonewall Jackson, of Va. 1824, Confederate general, defeated Banks at Cedar Mountain and captured 10,000 prisoners at Harper's Ferry '62, having reconnoitered with aids beyond his lines near Chancellorville he was taken for the approaching enemy and killed by his own troops.

Ben Johnson, 1574, 1637, English poet and dramatist, served as a mason, soldier, actor, author of 'Every Man in his humor,' 'Alchemist,' etc. Poet Laureate by James I.

Elisha Kent Kane, 1820, '57, Am. Artic explorer.

La Fayette, 1757, 1834, French general and patriot, aided America 1777, wounded at Brandywine, commander of French Nat. Guard, 1789, revisited Am. 1824 and prominent in French Revolution '30.

James Lawrence, 1781, 1813, Am. naval hero, commanded the Chesapeake, and killed by British frigate Shannon off Boston, exclaiming while dying "Don't give up the ship."

Robert E. Lee, of Va., 1806, '70, chief engineer of Scott's army in Mexico, commander in chief of the Confederate forces. Surrendered at Appomattox April 9, '65.

Henry W. Longfellow, of Maine, 1807, '82 poet, prof. of modern languages at Bowdoin '29, at Harvard '36, Hyperion, Hiawatha, Miles Standish, etc., among his works.

Ignatius de Loyola, 1491, 1566, Spanish founder of the Jesuits.

Martin Luther, of Eisleben, Germany, 1483, 1546, protestant reformer, priest 1507, prof. of philosophy at Wittenberg '08, denounced sale of indulgences '17, translated new testament '22 and old testament '34.

Thos. B. McCauley, 1800, '59, English historian, critic, and essayist.

Geo. B. McClellan, of Pa., 1826, '85, served in Mexican war, engineer lil. Cen. R. R. '57, commanded Federal forces '61, democratic candidate for presidency '64, afterwards governor of N. J.

Michael Angelo, 1474, 1563, greatest Italian painter, poet, sculptor, architect of St. Peters church at Rome.

John Milton, 1608, '74, greatest English poet, blind '54, completed 'Paradise Lost' '55.

Mahomet, A. D. 569, founder of the Moslem religion and author of the Koran.

Sir Thomas Moore, 1480, 1535, English statesman, philosopher, parliament 1504, author of Utopia '16.

Samuel F. B. Morse, 1791, 1872, Am. inventor of telegraph, constructed first line '44, Washington to Baltimore.

Horatio V. Nelson, 1758, 1805, greatest English naval commander, killed at Trafalgar where his fleet defeated French and Spanish.

Sir Isaac Newton, 1642, 1727, English philosopher and mathematician, discovered gravitation '67, author of 'Principia.'

Michael Ney, 1750, 1815, French marshal, was called 'bravest of the brave,' had five horses killed under him at battle of Waterloo, was captured afterwards and executed for treason.

GENERAL INFORMATION

William Pitt, 1759, 1806, English statesman and orator, parliament 1780, prime minister '83.

Thomas Paine, 1737, 1809, patriotical writer and free-thinker, author of 'The Crisis; 'Age of Reason,' etc.

Pocahontas, 1595, 1617, daughter of Chief Powhatan and saved life of Captain John Smith, married English gentleman Rolfe.

Israel Putnam, 1718, '90, Am. revolutionary general, prominent at Bunker Hill.

Pythagoras, B C 600, 510, Greek philosopher, taught the doctrine of transmigration of souls.

John Randolph, of Va., 1773, 1833, politician and orator, congress 1799, senate 1824, minister to Russia '30.

Peyton Randolph, of Va., 1723, 1775, president of the first American congress.

Jean Jaques Rousseau, 1712, '78, French philosopher and writer.

Johannes Schiller, 1759, 1805, most popular of German poets.

Sir Walter Scott, 1771, 1832, Scottish novelist and poet.

Wm. H. Seward, 1801, '72, secretary of state '61-9, nearly assassinated the same night that Lincoln was shot.

Horatio Seymour, 1811, '86, governor of N. Y. '52, reelected '62, democratic presidential candidate '68.

William Shakespeare, 1564, 1616, greatest English dramatist and famous author.

Philip H. Sheridan, 1831, general in Federal army and commander-in-chief, '83.

Henry W. Shaw, (Josh Billings) 1818, '85, American humorist.

John Sherman, 1823, Secretary of treasury 1877-81, resumed specie payment.

Wm. T. Sherman, 1820, Am. general, made the celebrated 'March to the Sea.' General of army '69.

Capt. John Smith, 1579, 1631, English explorer, founder of Va. first circumnavigator of the globe.

Charles H. Spurgeon, 1834, English pulpit orator and evangelist.

Alex. H. Stevens, of Ga. 1812, '83, statesman, congress '43, vice-president of the confederacy author of history U. S. and War between the States.

Thos. D. Talmage, 1832, noted preacher in New York city.

Samuel J. Tilden, 1814, '86, governor of N. Y., democratic candidate for president 1876, had popular majority of a quarter million, and was given by the 'electoral commission' 184 of the 369 electoral votes.

'Boss' Tweed, 1823, '78, politician, mayor of New York, and embezzler.

Matthew Vassar, 1792, 1868, founder of Vassar college.

Voltaire, 1694, 1778, French author poet, dramatist, historian, philosopher and skeptic.

James Watt, 1736, 1819, Scottish engineer and inventor, improved and completed steam engine.

Noah Webster, 1758, 1843, spent most of his life as a lexicographer.

Daniel Webster of N H, 1782, 1852, lawyer, orator, statesman, congress 1812, senate '28, secretary of ate, candidate for president '34.

Arthur W. Wellington 1769, 1852, Brittish general and statesman, parliament 1895, lost of Ireland '07, defeated Napoleon at Waterloo '15.

John G. Whittier of Mass, 1807, poet and author of famous ballads.

Wm. Wordsworth, 1770, 1850, English poet.

Ulrich Zwingle, 1484, 1531, Swiss reformer, killed in battle.

STANDING ARMIES.

Italy has an army of 214,000 and 2,175,000 trained men available. France keeps under arms 500,000 men, one-fourth cavalry, has 1850 field guns and 160 fortress batteries. Germany's land forces are 498,000 and she can muster about four times that number.—Austria's standing army numbers 289,000.—The English army 131,000, and in Brittish India 189,000. Its navy is 700 ships—The Russian Empire keeps standing 971,000 and and can muster in war time over 2,400,000—The Turkish standing army has 250,000 men—China has 300,000 soldiers. Our form of government makes it practicable to maintain peace with a very small force and we find the U S with only about 25,000 regular soldiers.

THE CIVIL WAR.

During the civil war from first to last 2,600,000 men were mustered in by the U. S. There were on duty Jan 1st, '61 14,663 Union soldiers, July '61 183,588, Jan '62, 527,204, Jan '63 698,802, Jan '64 611,250, Jan '65, 624,924. May '65, 797,807 and about one million on the muster rolls at the close of the war. Many of the Union soldiers were mustered in for short periods and none for a longer time than three years without re-enlistment.

The Confederate troops were mostly engaged during the war and at the close their army numbered but little over 150,000 although 600,000 had been on the muster rolls. The loss from battle on both sides was about 200,000 and from wounds, disease and subsequent deaths together with those totally disabled foots up nearly four times as many, thus making a sacrifice of nearly a million men and over eight billions of property, in one of the most remarkable civil wars the world has ever known.

MASON AND DIXON'S LINE.

A name given to the southern boundary line of the Free State of Pennsylvania which formerly seperated it from the Slave States of Maryland and Virginia. It was run—with the exception of about twenty-two miles—by Charles Mason and Jeremiah Dixon, two English mathematicians and surveyors, between Nov. 15, 1763, and Dec. 26, 1767. During the excited debate in Congress, in 1820, on the question of excluding slavery from Missouri, the eccentric John Randolph of Roanoke made great use of this phrase, which was caught up and re-echoed by every newspaper in the land, and thus gained a celebrity which it still retains.

NEW YORK AND BROOKLYN BRIDGE.

First talked of by Colonel Julius W Adams about 1865. Act of incorporation passed April, 1867. Survey begun by John A. Roebling, 1869. Construction begun January 2, 1870. First rope thrown across the river August 14, 1876. Master Mechanic Farrington crossed in a boatswain's chair August 25, 1876. Depth of the New York foundation below high water mark, 78 feet 6 inches. Depth of the Brooklyn foundation below high water mark, 45 feet. The New York tower contains 46,945 cubic yards of masonry; the Brooklyn tower, 38,214. Weight of the Brooklyn tower, about 22,052 tons. Weight of the New York tower, about a third more. Size of the towers at high water line 140x59 feet; at roof course 136x52 feet. Height of tower above high water 276 feet 6 inches. Height of roadway in the clear in the middle of the East River 135 feet. Grade of the roadway 3 feet 3 inches to 100 feet. Width of the promenade in the center of bridge 16 feet 7 inches. Width for railway on one side of the promenade 12 feet 10 inches. Width of carriage way on the other side of the promenade, 18 feet 9 inches. Width of bridge 85 feet. Length of main span 1,595 feet 6 inches. Length of each land span 930 feet

Length of the Brooklyn approach 971 feet. Length of the New York approach 1,560 feet. Length of each of the four great cables 3,578 feet 6 inches; diameter 15¾ inches; number of steel galvanized wires in each cable 5,434; weight of each cable about 870 tons. Ultimate strength of each cable 15,000 tons. Weight of steel in the suspended superstructure 10,000 tons. Total cost 15,000,000 dollars. Opened for traffic in 1883.

RAILWAY SUSPENSION BRIDGE, NIAGARA FALLS.

Engineer, John A. Roebling. Height of towers on American side 88 feet. Height of towers on Canada side 78 feet. Length of bridge 800 feet. Width of bridge 24 feet. Height above the river 250 feet. Number of cables 4. Diameter of cables 10 inches, containing about 4,000 miles of wire. Ultimate capacity of the 4 cables 12,400 tons. Total weight of bridge 800 tons. Distance between railway track and carriage road below 28 feet. Cost of construction 500,000 dollars. Bridge first opened for railway traffic March 8, 1855. Estimated depth of water in the channel beneath the bridge 250 feet. Velocity of current 20 miles per hour. Velocity of Whirlpool Rapids 27 miles per hour. Quantity of water passing through the gorge per minute 1,500,000,000 cubic feet.

NEW CAPITOL BUILDING AT ALBANY, N. Y.

It was decided to erect the New Capitol on the first day of May, 1865. On the ninth day of December, 1867, the work of excavation commenced and proceeded to a depth of sixteen feet below the surface. On the seventh day of July, 1869, the first stone in the foundation was laid. The corner stone was laid on the twenty-third day of June, 1871. The size is 300 feet north and south by 400 feet east and west, and with the porticos will cover three acres and seven square feet. The walls are 108 feet high from the water table. Total cost of the building up to February 25th, 1884 was $15,270,000. It is estimated that it will cost at least $5,000,000 more to complete it.

U. S. WEATHER SIGNALS.

White flag indicates clear or fair weather. Blue flag indicates rain or snow. Black triangular flag always refers to temperature; when placed above white or blue it indicates warmer weather; when placed below white or blue it indicates colder weather; when not displayed the indications are that the temperature will remain stationary, or that the change will not vary five degrees from the temperature of the same hour of the preceding day. White flag with black square in center, indicates the approach of a sudden and decided fall in temperature.

The weather predictions are issued at 1 a. m., daily for the twenty-four hours commencing at 7 a. m. These predictions are telegraphed to Signal Service stations, railroads, post-offices, etc.

The cold-wave warnings are telegraphed to the principal stations of the service from twenty-four to forty-eight hours in advance, when it is expected that the temperature will fall decidedly and suddenly.

HOW TO MEASURE CORN IN CRIB, ETC.

This rule will apply to a crib of any size or kind. Two cubic feet of good sound dry corn in the ear will make a bushel of shelled corn. Then to get the quantity of shelled corn in a crib of corn in the ear, measure the length breadth and height of the crib, inside of the rail, multiply the length by the breadth and the product by the height; then divide the product by two and you have the number of bushels of shelled corn in the crib.

To find the number of apples, potatoes, etc. in a bin, multiply the length breadth and thickness together, and this product by 8, and point off one figure in the product for decimals.

ANTIDOTES FOR POISONS

In case where the other articles to be used as antidotes are not in the house, give two tablespoonfuls of mustard mixed in a pint of warm water. Also give large draughts of warm milk or water mixed with oil butter or lard. If possible give as follows:

For bed-bug poison, blue vitriol, corrosive sublimate, sugar of lead, sulphate of zinc or red precipitate—give milk or white of eggs in large quantities.

For Fowler's solution or white precipitate, arsenic —give prompt emetic of mustard and salt—tablespoonful of each; follow with a quantity of sweet oil, butter or milk.

For antimonial wine or tartar emetic—drink warm water to encourage vomiting. If vomiting does not stop give a grain of opium as follows:

For oil vitriol, muriatic acid or oxalic acid—Magnesia or soap dissolved in water. Give every two minutes.

For caustic soda or caustic potash—drink freely of water with vinegar or lemon juice in it.

For carbolic acid—give flour and water or glutinous drinks.

For chloral hydrate or chloroform—pour cold water over the head and face, with artificial respiration, galvanic battery.

For carbonate of soda, copperas or cobalt—prompt emetic; soap or mucilaginous drinks.

For laudanum, morphine or opium—strong coffee followed by ground mustard or grease in warm water to produce vomiting. Keep in motion.

For nitrate of silver—give common salt in warm water.

For strychnine or tincture nux vomica—emetic of mustard or sulphate of zinc, aided by warm water.

REMEDIES FOR BURNS AND SCALDS.

Every family should have a preparation of flaxseed oil, chalk and vinegar, about the consistency of thick paint, constantly on hand for burns and scalds. The best application in cases of burns and scalds is a mixture of one part of carbolic acid to eight parts of olive oil. Lint or linen rags are to be saturated in the lotion, and spread smoothly over the burned part, which should then be covered with oil silk or gutta-percha tissue to exclude air.

STRENGTH OF ICE

Two inches thick—will support a man.
Four inches thick—a man on horseback.
Five inches thick—an eighty-pounder cannon.
Eight inches thick—a battery of artillery.
Ten inches thick—will support an army.

HOW TO MIX INK AND PAINTS FOR TINTS

Red and black makes..................Brown
Lake and white makes.................Rose
Umber and white makes................Drab
White and brown makes................Chestnut
Red with light blue makes............Purple
Blue with lead color makes...........Pearl
Carmine with white makes.............Pink
Lamp black with indigo makes........Silver Grey
Lamp black with white makes..........Lead color
Paris green with white makes.........Light green
Yellow ochre and white makes.........Buff
White tinted with purple makes......French white
Black with chrome green makes........Dark green
Emerald Green with white.............Brilliant green
Vermilion with chrome yellow.........Orange
Yellow with white lead...............Straw color
White tinted with red and yellow.....Cream
Yellow, blue, black and red..........Olive

COMPOSITION OF SOLDERS

Fine solder is an alloy of two parts of block tin, and one part of lead. Plumbing solder one part of block tin, two parts of lead. Glazing solder is equal parts of block tin and lead.

HYGIENE IN BRIEF.

Advice Worth Adhering to.

Always desiring to benefit our fellow-men whenever possible, we append the following hygienic rules, which after 20 years' experience as a physician and hygienist, we believe about covers the field:

First of all the foundation of good health should be started by correct living on the part of our parents before our birth, so that we may come into existence with an inborn constitution of stamina. In infant life, with strenuous effort, avoid the giving of any nostrums or much food of any kind, excepting that prepared by nature, or the simplest and plainest substitutes for it. Above all things do not begin to create a morbid taste by giving a *baby* tea, coffee, spices, fat meats, paregorics, soothing syrup, and the like all of which derange and destroy the nerve forces. As early as possible establish regular habits. A babe should have a sponge bath in the morning, a sun bath at noon, and a massage treatment before retiring. This latter, kneading of the muscles and gentle exercises of the limbs, prepares it for refreshing sleep. Even the time for nursing should be guaged by judgment and not by a child's cries. Beginning with two hours at the age of six months, it should be four hours between meal times, and solid food should never be taken by children or adults nearer than five hours nor oftener than three times a day. A habit once formed is very difficult to break, and as tobacco and strong drinks are certainly injurious, especially so before the system has come to full maturity, feed a child arsenic and strychnia in preference to tobacco, wine, or beer.

Every person should have plenty of exercise, plenty of pure air and sunlight, a proper observance of cleanliness, simple abstemious diet, and the avoidance of all licentiousness or extremes of any kind whatever. By regular exercise we do not mean work to fatigue for half an hour once a week; but if you are engaged in mental or sedentary employment, spend at least fifteen minutes three times a day in gymnastic or other proper exercise. Walking is good, riding is better, sawing or chopping wood is first-rate, and if you have no conveniences for any of these, you can, by a vigorous swinging of the arms, striking, kicking, etc., leaning forwards and backwards, take a sufficient gymnastic exercise in your bed-room without aid of dumb-bells or Indian clubs. This should certainly be done morning and evening, if you do not get sufficient exercise in some other manner, as you need the first to prepare your digestive powers for breakfast, and the latter to give refreshing sleep. Pure air and proper ventilation of rooms is absolutely necessary to health, and the naked exposure of the entire body to the sun is also very important to persons who do not get much out-of-door exercise. A comfortable room and south window at noontime are the requisites for this exhiliarating bath, rolling on the carpet and rubbing the surface of the body in order not to sunburn, but to keep up a brisk circulation. Every person should take a sponge or hand bath once, twice, or thrice a week in order to keep the millions of pores open. But few persons need this every day, and some may do well enough on once a week. Our habits are every second or third day, and a wash bowl and towel with a properly warmed bed-room and moderately cold water, serve our purpose most of the time as well as the bath tub; but in bathing as well as in diet, every person must, to some extent be a law unto themselves.

The matter of diet is an all important subject, and one in which it is very difficult to make absolute rules. There are, however, a few general rules which should be observed by every one. The process of mastication and digestion, ordinarily, requires from four to five hours, and the habit of piecing between meals, or taking a second meal before the first has full time for digestion and absorption, is extremely harmful, a great strain to the nerve power, and certain to end in impaired digestion. No person should do active mental or vigorous bodily labor for a few minutes prior to, and a full hour after, eating, as it draws upon the nerve power, which properly belongs to the digestive process. As to the kinds of food, it is an old and pertinent saying that what is wholesome for one person may be poisonous for another, so that every one must study their own idiosyncrasies. We however, believe that pork or lard in any manner is objectionable, being the cause of many of the skin diseases and bilious troubles; cucumbers or radishes have scarcely any nutriment, and are hard to digest; pastries, condiments, highly seasoned food, relishes, and conglomerate mixtures, as mince pies, ice cream, etcetera, are better left for those who are willing to sacrifice their health and endanger their lives for social customs, festivals, and late hours. Those who prefer health should eat corn bread graham bread, or light wheat bread, plain vegetable dishes, and sparingly of meats. Two or three kinds of food at a meal is infinitely better than a dozen or more. Eat slowly, masticate thoroughly, drink but little fluid, and that neither hot nor very cold. With these directions strictly followed, you will hardly be in danger of eating too much, but, of course, should not overload the stomach.

Go to bed at early hours; and to the ladies we will drop the old, old remark; do not constrain the waist, the feet or any part of the body, by tight lacing, tight shoes, or other impediment, that will interfere with free movement.

RAILROADS, ETC.
ROANOKE & SOUTHERN.
Country, Minerals, etc., of W'n in N.C.

An important feature of our pamphlet remains yet to be written, and one which we believe will enhance the future prospects of this place and the surrounding country as much, if not more, than any other agencies. A city with but a single railroad, however liberal that may be, cannot expect to command trade and succeed in miscellaneous manufacturing like a place with competing lines, stretching their iron arms to the various points of the compass to receive the traffic and transportation which their location and importance demand.

The Roanoke & Southern has been long talked about, and its great desirability as a cross line, extending to Roanoke, Va., on the north, and to some point in South Carolina on the south was acknowledged by every progressive citizen, but no active steps towards its speedy consummation had been made until quite recently. The Virginia and North Carolina construction company was formed in Winston in May last, a majority of the stock being held here, and recently this organization has taken the contract to build 60 miles of the road, from here to Martinsville, Va., upon which operations will be commenced at once, and it is expected that the line will be finished to that place within a year. The construction company also has an option on building the division from Martinsville to Roanoke, (55 miles), and the southern division as well. This company was incorporated with $50,000 capital stock, and with authority to increase the stock to $250,000 when necessary.

F. H. Fries, the Salem manufacturer, is president, and Jas. A. Gray, cashier of the Wachovia National Bank, the secretary and treasurer, with a number of the most solid business men in the Twin City as stockholders in the enterprise.

It is not our intention to soar into the poetical, but if you would see a land blessed with wealth of timber and minerals; with fertile valleys, sparkling waters and pure air, then come with us and travel over a space of about 60 miles through the beautiful Piedmont section of North Carolina.

After you cross the Virginia line, first you strike a ledge of soapstone which may be sawed into slabs as large as a barn door, and so free from grit that it can be dressed with a plane as smooth as marble. So useful and ornamental has it been found that it has been quarried and hauled by the citizens for miles around for hearthstones, mantels, etc. With transportation, this would furnish thousands of tons of freight.

A few miles on and you come to the mica. Many thousand pounds of this have been mined and hauled away. This bed extends over five miles on the line.

One mile further on you find lime, on Snow creek, which was at one time thought to be the finest marble in the state. Another mile southward, and you come to the regular magnetic iron belt. The ore from this range has been worked for nearly a hundred years, makes the best of iron, and is no doubt inexhaustible. Were it not for the dirt that has fallen in since they stopped work, owing to the introduction of rolled iron, twenty or thirty veins, from four to ten feet thick, assaying 45 to 70 per cent, metallic iron, would be shown. This is not in pockets, but in regular fissure veins, no one of which, so far as we are informed, ever cut out or failed in the working of nearly 100 years. This iron belt extends six miles, much of the way through the finest timber, to Danbury. Here the Dan river furnishes magnificent water power for any purpose. The ore, according to the analysis of Dr. Smith, is entirely free from phosphorous, and 2 tons specimens analyzed the lowest showed 49 and the highest 65 per cent, metallic iron.

Passing the six miles, you are at Danbury, a village noted for the healthfulness of its climate, with beautiful scenery on every side, while within a radius of five or six miles are at least twenty mineral springs, possessing valuable medicinal properties, which from May to November would bring not only hundreds, but thousands, of pleasure and health seekers.

Now we leave Danbury in the direction of Germanton, cutting right through a hill of magnetic iron and manganese at one mile, passing within half a mile of probably as fine granite as can be found in Greenwood cemetery. We cross the foot of Little Flatshoal creek and mountain, and find the real bed of manganese, an article used in the manufacture of steel rails, or Bessemer steel for other purposes, and which just at this time, is in very great demand, owing to the supplies running short in many places. This will furnish to the R. & S. R. R. tons of freight.

In the same neighborhood we find magnetic iron ore and graphite, almost pure plumbago. This is about six miles north from Germanton, all in the same neighborhood. Three miles further on are the different lime quarries, which have been worked for years.

Then we come to the coal on Town Fork, the veins of which at more than two or three places are 18 inches to 2½ feet thick, and not more than 15 feet from the surface.

Crossing the line into Forsyth, you have lime and a heavy deposit of serpentine, that in the near future will furnish many tons of freight to the Roanoke & Southern Railroad.

Between this and Winston are many outcrops of iron, manganese, limestone, and other minerals, whose extent has never been investigated, and whose richness has never been tested. There is considerable iron at

Brown's Creek, while a little to the north and east, 18 miles from Winston-Salem is an outcrop of coal, which is thought to be invaluable and inexhaustible. The State of North Carolina has appropriated $1,000 for developing these coal fields, and a mining expert is investigating them.

All over this section, says Judge Kelly, of Pennsylvania, there are ores, the finest his eyes ever rested on, minerals, timbers and water powers that ought and will make this the beautiful Piedmont section, one of the richest and most prosperous countries in the world. All it needs is capital, and this it will get as soon as capitalists know its resources.

Some of this section may be west of the route followed by the Roanoke & Southern, but most of it will be tributary at least to that road, and in addition to valuable minerals, it has thousands of acres of fertile valleys yet undeveloped, and which good transportation facilities would cause to be developed at once.

The construction and completion of the Roanoke & Southern will bring many small miscellaneous manufacturing enterprises here, and these assist greatly in the prosperity of any city. Winston-Salem is progressive, and every indication points to a bright future and continued prosperity. We believe that no better time for investment in real estate ever presented than the present, and if you desire a residence or manufacturing site the Twin City presents many advantages. The professional and mercantile departments are well represented already.

LIVERY STABLES.
CRUTCHFIELD & McARTHUR.
Church Street Livery.

The livery business is not so absolutely essential to public progress as are railroads, but they are a great convenience, and Winston, as other live cities, has a full quota of liveries. E. G. Crutchfield was born in Orange county, and served as conductor for six years after the road was first opened to Salem. Eight years ago he opened the livery, and two years later accepted R. M. McArthur, of Virginia, as partner. The firm have a fine brick stable, run the transfer line to all trains, and are fully equipped throughout.

BARHAM & HOLLAND.
Livery, Feed and Sale Stable.

Barham & Holland opened up in the livery business in February, 1887, and keep from eight to twelve horses, the usual line of buggies, carriages, phaetons, etc. N. B. Barham is son of the well known auctioneer at Brown's warehouse, and familiar with horses for many years. John W. Holland was born in Forsyth, but has spent most of his life in agricultural pursuits in Davidson county. Good turnouts are always at the call of customers.

J. M. ROBINSON.
Livery and Sale Stable.

J. M. Robinson was reared in Clinton county, and five years since established the livery, sale and feed business in Winston. His stables are on Third street, between Church and Chestnut, where he keeps from eight to ten horses, and all the requisites of livery, besides purchasing and selling all kinds of desirable horses to meet the wants of customers or the demands of trade.

The roads in the vicinity of the Twin-City are being macadamized and recently a new bridge has been put across Salem Creek. Geo. H. Craft of Atlanta, Ga., was awarded the contract for the building, while the work was done under the supervision of J. A. McCorkle. The material was furnished by the Smith Bridge Co., of Toledo, Ohio, the total cost of the bridge and all work connected with its construction was $1,419.17. The approaches to the bridge on either side for some distance is being nicely macadamized with crushed granite.

SALEM MERCHANDISE, ETC.

W. P. ORMSBY,
Organs, Pianos, Sewing Machines.

Wm. P. Ormsby is a native of England, has been a resident of this city for 14 years, and some two years ago engaged in the sale of the popular Domestic Sewing Machines, of which he has placed over 800 in the homes of Forsyth and surrounding counties. This machine is simple in its construction, easy to manage and wide in its range of work. Its proprietors have taken great pains to produce a first class machine in all respects, and twenty years of practical use have demonstrated its superiority in many respects over other competitors. Mr. Ormsby keeps needles and supplies for all kinds of machines, and has facilities for repair work. He is a practical musician, playing 1st violin in the Salem Orchestra. He sells everything in pianos, organs or musical goods, doing tuning and repairing as well. Mr. Ormsby makes a specialty of the Estey, Palace, and Kimball organs, the Stieff, Wheelock and other pianos although any desirable style or make is furnished to suit the order of the customer.

FRIES, GIERSH & SENSEMAN,
General Merchandise.

One of the largest mercantile houses in Salem is that mentioned above. H. W. Fries the senior partner is well known in manufacturing. H. A. Giersh is a native of Salem, six years a merchant and in '87 became a partner as above. Mr. Senseman is in the stove trade as noticed elsewhere. The firm keeps a full line of general merchandise and does a leading trade. The firm keeps a full line of Ziegler Brothers popular manufacture of fine shoes, for men, women and children's wear, and the sales for the past twelve months show a large advance over previous years. Fries, Giersh and Senseman have a considerable jobbing trade but give special attention to their large retail business, occupying three stories with their wares and are the leading house in Salem merchandise.

CLINARD & BROOKES,
Dry Goods, Groceries and Notions.

L. N. Clinard is a native of Davidson Co. and his partner, C. B. Brookes, from Forsyth Co. but both are old residents of the place. Mr. Clinard having for 19 years been in the office of Messrs. Fries and Mr. Brookes having been in the revenue service and in merchandising as one of the firm of Reed Brothers & Brookes.

A year ago the present co-partnership was formed for the conduct of general merchandise, of which they carry a good assortment under that general heading, and their first year of sales has largely exceeded the expectations of Messrs. Clinard & Brookes.

D. A. SPAUGH,
Grocery and Livery Stable.

D. A. Spaugh is a native of Davidson county, and has been in trade at Salem for fourteen years. Mr. S. keeps a full line of groceries and a stock of general merchandise. He makes large shipments of fresh fruits and produce, and is a progressive merchant.

At his livery stable in rear of Hunter block Mr. Spaugh keeps seven to ten good horses and a full outfit of buggies, carriages, phaetons, etc. His merchandise trade is principally retail, but he does a fair line of jobbing of well.

W. O. SENSEMAN & CO.,
Stoves, Tinware, Etc.

Stoves, tin, and sheet iron merchandise has been conducted at the sign of the Big Coffee Pot in Salem for the past quarter of a century, and three years ago it was purchased by Giersh, Senseman & Co., the senior partner retiring from the trade, with Jan. '88

ries the firm name as above. H. E.
Fries being the "Co." Tobacco flues
are one of the specialties of the firm
and tin ware at wholesale and retail. A line of grates, heaters, cook-
stoves and house goods are kept
by the firm and the wants of the customers carefully looked after.

W. & E. PETERSON.
Cabinet Shop—Salem.

Karsten Peterson, of Denmark,
came to the Southern States in 1806
as a missionary to the Indians.
About ten years later he located in
Salem, and opened up the cabinet
trade in a store house that had been
built a quarter of a century before,
and this, although having seen the
storms of a hundred winters, is still
occupied by W. & E. Peterson, the
former being past 75 years of age
and still working with the saw and
plane on the spot where he was born.

H. W. SHORE.
Groceries and Confectionery.

H. W. Shore was born in this vicinity and has lived in Salem over 35
years. He was for a long time a clerk
in the post-office and served for thirteen years as postmaster. In Dec.
'82 he opened his stock of merchandise at the corner of Main and New
Shallowford St. where he keeps a full
line of family and fancy groceries,
queensware, confectioneries and cigars. Mr. Shore has a large acquaintance throughout the county.

MRS. T. E. DOUTHIT.
Millinery and Fancy Goods.

For 20 years Mrs. T. E. Douthit
has administered to the millinery
wants of Salem and right well has
she done this, to hold a large share
of the custom in that line in a city of
this size. Mrs. D. is an experienced
milliner and also keeps expert hands
in the custom department. The line
of ribbons, fancy goods etc. is extensive, and she is to be congratulated
upon 20 years of successful trade.

MERCANTILE INTERESTS.

Winston-Salem is a central point
for a large section of country, Salem
having before the days of a railroad
been a mercantile town of large importance, while Winston of more recent and rapid development now
takes the lead in merchandising. The
superior richness and flavor of fruits
grown in this section has made for
us an extensive dried fruit demand
and in an exceptionally good year
more than 100 car loads, aggregating over two million pounds have
been shipped from the Twin-City to
the northern and western markets.
The average yield is 40 car loads of
dried apples, 20 of peaches, and 30
or more of blackberries, pears, cherries, raspberries, huckleberries, etc.

There are always those who are
willing to look on the dark side and
decry our progress. While the building boom of Winston two or three
years since may have been pushed beyond a healthy growth, an intimate
acquaintance with the leading merchants and manufacturers, warrants
us in saying that business is steadily
increasing and the output of 1888
will show a decided improvement on
that of last year. This place has
more than a hundred mercantile
firms and as our work is now on its
last third we shall necessarily skip
some minor concerns and make very
brief reference to others. We do not
claim it to be a complete index, but
hope to give a fair representation to
all houses of special prominence and
we do no injustice to others by starting with one of the oldest houses in
trade as it is also among the
largest. It is our purpose to give
merited prominence in the various
lines of trade to those houses which
add most to the importance of the
city as a trade center.

The postage on these pamphlets
will be 2 cents each. Mail them to
your friends and customers.

HINSHAW & MEDEARIS,
General Wholesale and Retail Merchants.

The above firm are deserving of a liberal space as this house has long been identified with the development of Winston, the senior partner now being one of the oldest merchants in the place. Harman Miller, Robert Gray, Sullivan & Bell, William Barrow, F. L. Gorrell, Holder & Faircloth, Hodgin & Sullivan and some smaller firms had preceded Mr. Hinshaw, but Winston had less than 500 inhabitants when he commenced trade here in 1870. He is a native of Chatham county and came to this place in 1867.

The firm style was Hinshaw & Co. at first and has since made several changes. The present large structure was erected by Hinshaw Brothers about ten years ago, has three floors 70x70, comprising eleven apartments all well filled. Two elevators are in use and as it is easier to tell what the firm does not keep than to give their long list of wares we will simply say that everything that comes under the head of general merchandise, (clothing and millinery alone excepted,) is found in the wholesale and retail emporium of Hinshaw & Medearis. N. H. Medearis is a native of Forsyth county, began as salesman in the house ten years ago and last year became a partner. Mr. Hinshaw as before noted has taken an interest in the tobacco development from its incipiency he having fitted up the first ware room for tobacco sales. He was prominent in the first movement for a graded school, has been connected with the city government and as chairman of the committee on internal improvement has taken an active part in the development of railroads. This firm in company with F. & H. Fries, and by the assistance of display room from Col. Gorrell, for three years conducted a wheat and cattle fair in Winston.

In addition to an extensive retail trade in all general lines of goods the firm of Hinshaw & Medearis do a large jobbing trade for a radius of a hundred miles or more from Winston. Their aggregate sales reaching about $250,000. The firm gives employment to a dozen hands, carries $35,000 to $50,000 in stock, purchases large quantities of produce and dried fruits and from its liberal and progressive spirit contributes a full share towards the importance of Winston as a commercial center.

W. T. CARTER & CO.,
Dry Goods, Groceries, Fertilizers etc.

Sagacity and good judgment is as certainly necessary for commercial success as it is for professional or manufacturing prosperity statistics show that more than one half of all who engage in mercantile pursuits fail or abandon the business during the first five years of trade. W. T. Carter began merchandising in 1874 and nine years ago moved to Winston. Five years since he consolidated with Brown & Carter, of warehouse fame, in the present mercantile venture. A complete line of dry goods, groceries, millinery, notions, etc., at wholesale or retail is found here, large assortment of fine shoes, gents furnishing goods, in fact all the requirements of trade, clothing and hardware excepted. The firm occupy a finely lighted room in Brown's Opera House block, corner of Main and Fourth streets, having a large basement storage and two warehouses. They are extensive dealers in fertilizers keeping this product as well as other heavy storage in their railroad warehouse. Messrs. Carters and Brown are among our most influential citizens and the firm is solid in every respect. The partners have largely been interested in developing the commercial interest of Winston and the transactions of the house compare favorably with other leading mercantile establishments.

DESCRIPTIVE SKETCH

The house of Vaughn & Pepper may well be classed among our leading merchants and its rapid increase in trade is a sure indication of the elevated commercial standard on which the operations are based. J. B. Vaughn is a native of Rockingham county and began business in Winston as one of the firm of Vaugh & Prather some 14 years ago. Later, with Maj. Brown he started the hardware business now conducted by Brown, Rogers & Co., and about five years since in company with T. R. Pepper of Stokes county, for many years merchandising in Danbury, the present business was entered into. The firm at first occupied the Ogburn corner, but their buiness had a rapid increase and a year ago they completed the fine brick structure of which we give a correct illustration above. The building is 30x90 fronting on Liberty and having an entrance on Fourth street. The first floor is occupied with the retail trade, and it is a dull day indeed, when the clerks are not busy here. The second and third floors are entirely taken up with the wholesale trade while the basement is used for heavy storage. A warehouse in the rear and another near the depot are filled with their merchandise. The output of business the first year was about $25,000 and that of 1888 will probably be ten fold that amount showing a phenomenal increase for five years of trade. A dozen persons find employment and the firm does a flourishing retail and jobbing business throughout western North Carolina.

General Merchandise at Wholesale and Retail.

J. E. GILMER.
An Exclusive Wholesale House.

Winston has a number of jobbing houses in connection with the retail business, but as yet has only one house devoted exclusively to the wholesaling of general merchandise and that is the above. Capt. J. E. Gilmer is a native of Greensboro, and commenced the mercantile trade in 1867. Fifteen years since he came to Winston and opened up a stock of general merchandise, doing both a retail and jobbing trade. The wholesale business soon became a prominent feature, and in 1884 he closed up the retailing and turned his attention entirely to jobbing. From time to time the Captain has built additional room, until his store now fronts 55 feet on Main street and his last structure has both basement and upstairs room, besides a large warehouse for heavy groceries on the rear end of the lot. A full assortment of groceries, provisions, dry goods, shoes, trunks and everything coming under the head of general merchandise is carried by this house, the trade reaches out over Western, N. C. and adjacent counties in other states. We have previously mentioned Capt. Gilmer as a partner in the Orinoco warehouse and in the firm of Edmunds & Gilmer leaf dealers. He is one of Winston's progressive merchants, whose enterprise and business tact has brought him to the front and his various interests are important factors in the general welfare of the city.

ROSENBACHER BROS.,
Dry Goods Clothing and Furnishing.

The separation of different lines of trade is an enterprise that enables a firm to carry a larger and more complete assortment in a special branch and give closer attention to its details, and the above firm has done its share towards the division of the various lines of trade in this city. Three separate stores are conducted by this house. The clothing and gents' furnishing house occupies the double front Buxton building 40x85 feet and is said to be the largest room and best assortment of clothing to be found in the state of North Carolina, comprising all sizes and qualities demanded in the trade. Two rooms of the fine Gray block, 25x85 each, and communicating by an archway, are filled with a complete assortment in their lines. One department comprises dry goods, carpets and millinery, the other is devoted to hats and shoes exclusively. The shoe store is thoroughly filled with everything desirable in foot wear. We cannot go into the minutia of this extensive concern, but will simply say that Rosenbacker Bros. are shrewd buyers, are fully alive to the interests of their customers and there is nothing that a lady could desire in dry goods, domestics or notions but what they endeavor to keep. A dozen clerks find employment in these three stores and a large business is transacted. The partners are of German nativity and in trade at Arcola four years prior to engaging in the trade of this place in 1880.

BEE HIVE CASH STORE.
W. D. Baity & Sons, Proprietors.

It has long been an established fact that mercantile houses based strictly upon the cash system can afford to sell goods at a closer margin than credit stores, as they have no bad debts to cut down the average percentage, save the time of a book keeper, collector and loss of interest on delayed payments. Such firms usually purchase, as well as to sell, for spot cash, thus securing good bargains and saving heavy discounts. To some dealers the establishment of a strictly cash business appears impracticable but the large trade of the Bee Hive Cash Store which was opened in the Buxton-Shelton block on Main Street opposite the Court house, by W. D. Baity & Sons, of Yadkin county, April first of this year, is a sufficient evidence that people who pay cash appreciate these advantages. This firm has long been conducting a store in Yadkin county and have recently closed that out in order to put their entire energy and capital in the enterprise at this place. Their stock is one of the general merchandise, which receives daily additions in order to keep it fully up to the requirements. The three months of trade here has fully reached the most sanguine expectation of the partners and W. D. Baity & Sons are welcomed to the Twin-City as men whose live spirit of business will advance our commercial interests.

J. TISE & CO.
General Merchandise House.

Jacob Tise was born in Davidson county but located here before Winston was commenced. Mr. Tise was one of the early mayors of Winston and in 1865 in company with S. A. Ogburn he began merchandising as Tise & Ogburn. Changes have been made in the firm several times, but Mr. J. Tise still remains, with C. H. Tise now as managing partner. Jacob Tise erected the row of a half dozen stores from the original room on the corner of Main and Fourth street to and including the fine galvanized iron front which bears his name. This store of general merchandise does a large trade and has been in business for 23 years. C. H. Tise has been connected with the house from boyhood. He is the patentee of an improved well fixture which has become very popular in this section from its great convenience and absolute safety for children to handle. Mr. Tise should make a fortune on this if its merits were fully known. There are thousands now in use and room for hundreds of thousands more. Manufacturers would do well to correspond with him if they desire to produce a useful and good selling article.

D. S. REID.
General Merchandise.

Among our large dealers in general merchandise the name of D. S. Reid should have a prominent mention. Mr. R. is a native of Guilford county, came to this place eleven years ago and began merchandising. The business has had a steady increase from the first and to accommodate his large stock in trade, the convenient two story brick 25x95 feet at the corner of main and second streets was built by him and first occupied in Jan. 1885. This has an elevator and other conveniences. Mr. Reid holds an extensive retail trade and does a fair share of jobbing. The stock comprises everything usually classed under the head of general merchandise, clothing and millinery alone excepted. A warehouse for storage of fertilizers, in which he has a large trade, adjoins the railroad track and Mr. Reid has gained a wide city and country custom in his eleven years of trade here.

RACKET STORE
And Cheap John's Quarters.

D. D. Schouler, proprietor of both the above houses was brought up in the mercantile trade of New York city and five years ago located in this place. He keeps a large line of dry goods, millinery, fancy goods, notions and stationery next door to the post-office, a few months since on account of his extensive ladies' trade having removed the gents' furnishing, clothing and goods in that line to a store room across the street in the Liberty block whereauction sales are conducted every night. The dry goods house is furnished with the elevated cash system, the counter sunk unique show case plan, and is conveniently arranged throughout. Mr. Schouler is well satisfied with his success in Winston and has invested in real estate and buildings to the improvement of this place.

THORNTON & CO.,
General Merchandise.

R. L. Thornton is a native of Washington, N. C., and was in mercantile pursuits there for several years. He was for a time in the mill business at New Berne, coming from there to Winston in 1885. Mr. Thornton bought out the stock of J. F. Prather in the Bitting block, made large additions, and his salesroom, 26x90, is filled with everything that goes to make up a general merchandise stock, hardware alone excepted. To many persons it is a decided convenience, to be able to purchase their dry goods, staple and fancy groceries, boots, shoes, hats and clothing in the same establishment. Mr. T. not only keeps these, but crockery, house-furnishing goods, anything for men, women or children's wear, and the endless variety of notions so essential in the family.

JOE. JACOBS.
Main Street Clothier.

Born in Prussia, Joseph Jacobs emigrated to America in 1869 and was in the clothing trade at different places prior to locating in Winston about a dozen years ago. By integrity and intelligent business dealing Mr. Jacobs has ascended the ladder of mercantile fame until he holds a high position and carries a good stock in all the lines of men's, boys' and youths' clothing as well as a general line of gents' furnishing goods, jewelry etc. Mr. J. has served Winston faithfully as a commissioner and been honored with a reelection to the office. His rooms are at the corner of Main and Third streets in the business center of the city.

H. A. WATKINS & BRO.,
Dry Goods, Shoes and Groceries.

H. A. Watkins & Bro. are both natives of Davidson county, the senior partner having commenced merchandising in Lexington ten years ago and been for six years past in the trade of Winston. Jos. J. Watkins, a teacher for many years in Davie and Yadkin counties has recently purchased an interest in the establishment and the firm title has been changed to the above. H. A. Watkins & Bro. keep a good outlay of dry goods and clothing and are just preparing to add a full line of groceries for the accommodation of their customers. The house is on Main street near second.

H. A. HESTER & SON.
General Stores.

H. A. Hester is a native of this county, has been 15 years in trade and with the present year accepted his son as a partner in the business. They have a stock of merchandise on North Liberty street, Winston, and have recently established a store at the lower end of Main street, Salem, thus being prepared to capture the trade from either direction.

W. L. FRANKLIN & CO..
Shoe and Notion House.

W. L. Franklin is a native of Carteret county, and has been three years merchandising here, having been in the trade for half a dozen years at Durham prior to coming to this place. The firm occupy a double front store on Liberty street, and keep a full stock of shoes and hats, besides an endless variety of notions.

FULLER & DURHAM.
Drygoods, Notions, Etc.

T. S. Fuller is a native of Franklin county, and came from Raleigh here in 1884. I. W. Durham is noticed elsewhere as a marble dealer. The firm have been in business since April, 1886, and occupy the granite front Stein block, with their assortment of drygoods, shoes, hats, etc.

CLARKE & FORD.
Dry Goods, Groceries, Etc.

Both Virginians, and commenced in the trade of Winston in 1875, at the corner, which was first used in merchandise by Harman Miller shortly after the village was started. Clark & Ford keep a general stock of merchandise, and have done a fairly successful trade.

Hardware, Stoves, Etc.

BROWN, ROGERS & CO.,
Hardware, Machinery, Agr'l Impl's.

Vaughn, Brown & Carter under the firm name of Vaughn & Co., started the hardware business in 1878 and eight years ago J. M. Rogers purchased the interest of Vaughn and the business has since been run as Brown, Rogers & Co. Mr. Rogers is from Charleston, S. C., and Messrs Brown & Carter are our well-known warehouse men. The firm have a double front store under the Opera House and a large basement to the same. The building is 90 feet deep and the outlay in all lines of hardware is complete, the business having been greatly extended under Mr. Rogers' management. A splendid assortment of stoves is kept and just at present special attention is directed to the Gauze Door Range which has many features of merit for roasting, baking etc. Agricultural implements and farming machinery embrace a large part of their business. Geiser threshers, horse powers, grain drills, McCormick mowers and binders, steam engines, r r supplies, belting, Wadsworth's Silicia paints (used by the U. S. Government,) white lead and oils are sold by them. A large and varied stock of buggies and all kinds of carriage material are found here and the special wants of the farming community have been considerately cared for by Brown, Rogers & Co. in the make up of their large stock.

R. R. CRAWFORD.
Hardware, Farming Machinery, Etc.

R. R. Crawford was born in Rowan county reared in Charlotte and since the war had been in the hardware trade at Salisbury until he removed to Winston in 1883. Mr. Crawford has given special care to the requirements of the farming community and is widely known in Western N. C., his trade in machinery, agricultural implements, farmers' supplies and house furnishing goods extending over Forsyth and adjoining counties. In grain machinery he makes a specialty of the well known Deering Twine Binder, keeping also the Deering and Meadow King Mowers.

The business occupies four floors in the Ogburn corner, at Fourth and Liberty streets having a double salesroom on the first floor. In addition to machinery and general hardware. Mr. Crawford keeps wagons, buggies, carriages, supplies, mechanics' tools, sporting goods and the endless variety of sundries which go to make up a first-class hardware establishment. Institutions of this magnitude attract business to our city and assist in making the Twin-City an important commercial center.

S. E. ALLEN.
Hardware and Crockery.

S. E. Allen is a native of Granville county and has been in trade at this place since 1876. His accommodations and stock are much the same as the two above houses, with the addition of crockery. Since compiling our article on Electric Light, Capt. Allen has been elected as secretary of the company. He is also secretary and treasurer of the Piedmont Springs Company which has been formed with the design of advertising the fine chalybeate waters in Stokes county.

G. STEWART.
Tin Manufacturing and Stoves.

Is a native of England, in America from childhood, and five years in his present business. He keeps stoves and manufactures any kind of tin and sheet iron ware. He also does roofing, spouting and the whole line of trade.

Drugs, Paints and Sundries.

DR. V. O. THOMPSON.
Drugs, Paints and Drug Sundries.

Dr. V. O. Thompson is from Warren county, N. C. He graduated from the University of Penna in 1859 and served as assistant surgeon in the late war, returning to Warren county where he practiced for several years. Jan. 1st 1874 Dr. Thompson commenced in the drug trade of Winston was burned out Dec. '79, rebuilt in 1880 and in just one year from his first conflagration suffered the second loss by fire. He then purchased his present stand on the street opposite the Court house where he keeps a full line of drugs, medicines, paints and sundries in all their varieties. Dr. Thompson has an elegant wall soda apparatus which cost $1,500 and in which the combination of foreign marbles gives a highly artistic effect. Dr. Thompson is the oldest druggist in Winston and his store has always been kept up to the requirements of trade, containing everything usually found in a first-class drug store. John Bynum has been chief clerk in the house for many years.

ASHCRAFT & OWENS,
Drugs, Medicines, Paints, Sundries.

H. C. Ashcraft is a native of Monroe, Union county, N. C. and has been in the drug trade for twelve years. B. B. Owens is a Pennsylvanian eight years a druggist and three years since began clerking for Gray & Martin. A year later in company with Mr. Ashcraft, purchasing the present business. There are but four drug stores in the Twin-City and this fact enables all of them to keep a full stock thus accommodating the public better than a half dozen or more smaller stores would do. Ashcraft & Owens are both practical men and study the requirements of their trade so the assortment in drugs, chemicals, sundries, lead oil and paint goods in general is kept filled up to the demand while special care is given to filling prescriptions. The usual soda fountain and other etceteras are found and with the completion of the Wachovia bank corner the firm will have an elegant room in the form of an L fronting both on Main and Third streets.

BROWN & BROWN,
Druggists and Opera House Lessees.

Smith & Brown fitted up the commodious drug rooms near the corner Fourth and Liberty streets in 1882 and a year since F. C. Brown purchased the interest of Capt. Smith making the firm name Brown & Brown. The Browns are both natives of Davie county, N. C. having come to Winston in 1872 and in 1880 engaged with Capt. Smith in the drug enterprise. F. C. Brown has long been principal salesman with W. T. Carter & Co. The store is finely fitted up having handsome shelf ware, soda fountain, etc. The management is in the hands of W. C. Brown whose long service in business leaves it unnecessary for us to add further comment. This firm also has the management of Brown's Opera House.

Jewelry Stores.

W. T. VOGLER.
Watches, Clocks, Jewelry, Etc.

Phillip Christopher Vogler, born in 1725 in Palatinate, come to this vicinity from Broad Bay, Maine, in 1779 and from him the Voglers of Forsyth county descended. John Vogler commenced the Watchmakers trade in Salem about 1800 and this and the Gunsmith trade were favorite occupations of the family. Wm. T. Vogler learned both and has been in the jeweler's business for 23 years. In 1879 Mr. Vogler became convinced that Winston would make the center of trade and removed his jewelry business here, still retaining a residence in Salem. The location is on Main street opposite the Merchants hotel and the store is well worth a visit as it contains a large stock in all departments of the jewelry trade and is handsomely fitted up. It has 8 nickel showcases, two common, and one superb wall case which was manufactured by A. C. Vogler in Salem at a cost of over $150. This is a model of elegance and convenience and is filled with fine silverware, etc. The outlay of clocks, watches, jewelry and optical goods is very large and all the requirements of a complete jewelry house is found here. Mr. Vogler is assisted in the store and repair department by his son Henry and W. E. Lineback. The establishment from its commencement here has merited and enjoyed the patronage of our best citizens.

JOSEPH BEVAN.
Watchmaker and Jeweler.

Joseph Bevan commenced the watchmaker's trade in his native city of Baltimore in 1840, and still puts in his time faithfully at the bench. Four years ago he moved from Williamsport to this city and opened up an attractive salesroom on Main street, where he keeps a well selected stock of clocks, watches and jewelry.

Millinery Stores.

MRS. STANTON & MERRITT.
Millinery and Fancy Goods.

Mrs. Stanton commenced the millinery trade in this city in 1879, and three or four years later erected the building now occupied by the firm nearly opposite Hotel Fountain. Mrs. Merritt became a partner in the trade some five years ago, and the firm keep a very complete stock in the millinery and fancy goods line. The cases and shelves are filled with a superb outlay of hats, ribbons, flowers and feathers; laces, trimmings and fancy goods in general. The trimming department is handsomely lighted, and any desirable style of ladies' head-gear is furnished to the order of customers.

MRS. A. S. MASTEN.
Millinery Store.

Ada S. Masten is a native of this State, residing in New York for some time, and is an experienced milliner and trimmer. She opened up a stock of goods in her present commodious rooms opposite Merchant's Hotel, April, 1888, and has already secured quite a large patronage. Mrs. Masten keeps some fancy goods, everything desirable in millinery, and endeavors to reproduce New York styles in trimming. Her rooms are in the business center of the city, on Main street, near the Wachovia bank corner.

Ice, Coal, Confect's, Groceries, Etc

D. H. KING.
Coal, Ice, and Bottling Works.

In 1882 D. H. King, of Richmond, Va., opened up the ice and coal trade in the Twin-City. He erected suitable storage buildings, sheds and scales, at the corner of Third and Depot streets adjoining the railroad and at once commanded a good trade. Mr. King has convenient delivery wagons and is prepared to assist his people in keeping warm or cool, as circumstances may demand. He handles the anthracite coal of Shamokin, Pa., the bituminous of Pocahontas, Va., Black Diamond, of Tennessee and Cumberland coal of Maryland. He purchases the Kennebec ice from his mother, Mrs. Jane King, who is an extensive dealer in Richmond Va. Mr. King is abreast of the times in all his methods giving our people the accommodations of large cities in these respects. A couple of years since he purchased the confectionery business of A. H. Potter, on Main street opposite the Merchants Hotel, where a large assortment of confectioneries is to be found at all times. The establishment has a handsome soda fountain and ice cream parlors connected therewith. A year since Mr. K. purchased a bottling apparatus and puts up, for the wholesale trade, mineral waters, soda flavors and the popular Vienna Cabinet and Tivoli beers. Altogether Mr. King is one of the stirring business men who assist in making this a live city.

F. B. EFIRD.
Fancy and Staple Groceries.

A house confining itself closely to one line of trade, is able to make a special study of that branch and F. B. Efird located here Jan. 1886 and has given his entire attention to staple and fancy groceries. The result has been highly satisfactory to the proprietor and it is only proper to say that he conducts one of the leading grocery houses of Winston. It is not surpassed for neatness attractiveness or completeness of assortment. He does a considerable jobbing trade in confectioneries cigars and fancy groceries; but in heavy stock, as flour, hams, etc., carries only what is required for the local trade. Mr. Efird has built up a rapid and successful trade in his two years of stay in this place.

H. J. WILLIAMS & CO.,
Bakers and Grocers.

Bread is the staff of life and every city must needs have its bakery. The above firm has recently commenced business at the corner of Fourth and Main streets and are delivering to customers anywhere in the city, fresh bread, cakes and pies every morning. H. J. Williams is a native of R. I. removing to Virginia 25 years ago and for 12 years past at Greensboro. G. J. Starr is of English descent and well known to our people. The firm besides bakery and confectionery goods keeps groceries and produce in general.

J. G. YOUNG.
Merchandise Broker.

Maj. J. G. Young was raised in Charlotte, N. C. and for eight years was connected with the transportation department of the Piedmont Air Line. He located in Winston five years ago in the brokerage business represents the packing house of Armour & Co., of Chicago, in meats, lard, etc., deals extensively in grain, flour and coal, the annual transactions averaging about $100,000 and making an important output of Winston.

J. F. FULTON.
Merchandise Broker.

Is a native of Stokes county, came to Winston in 1885, was salesman for D. S. Reid and Maj. Young prior to engaging in the brokerage and commission business in 1887. Mr. Fulton represents the Chicago Packing and Provision Company, and deals in lard, meat, provisions and grain with monthly sales amounting to nearly $5,000. His office is next door to Hinshaw & Medearis and the warehouses for the business are near the railroad depot

J. S. GRUBB.
Groceries, Vegetables, Etc.

Was born in this vicinity and raised in farming. He took charge of the city water works pumps in 1883, and has since been at that post. At the old Belo foundry site he has a fine garden planted out, and in his store, recently opened up on Liberty street, will sell largely of vegetables of his own product, besides general groceries. Mr. G. has 1,000 watermelon plants growing, 6,000 cabbages, and various other products.

J. F. HARRIS.
Groceries, Provisions, Produce.

A native of Iredell county, J. F. Harris came to this city a dozen years ago and for six years clerked for J. Tise. In 1883 Mr Harris commenced trade for himself, and a couple of years since he secured the fine brick corner at 4th and Chestre ts where he keeps a good assortment in the grocery line, giving special attention to the handling of country produce.

THE CITY PANTRY.
D. D. Paylor, Manager.

Was opened in April last, at the corner of Sixth and Old Town streets. Mr. Paylor is of Caswell county, formerly in the grocery trade, and for ten years past a book-keeper for different firms of this place. His stock is select family groceries.

C. A. WINKLER.
Baker, Confectioner, Etc.

Is a native of Salem and commenced trade there in 1866, ten years later he started a branch business in

Winston and still conducts both houses. He has a bakery with all its requisites, keeps a full assortment of confectioneries and manufactures his plain candies. He is an extensive manufacturer of ice cream, keeps a restaurant; beer, and oysters in season.

N. T. WATKINS.
Dry Goods and Shoes.

A native of Halifax county, Va., N. T. Watkins commenced business here 13 years ago, and has recently decided to retire from trade. He has yet quite a full stock in dry goods and shoes which he is closing out at cost to go out of business, and offers bargains in everything which he has for sale.

A. HUBAND.
Grocer and Confectioner.

Was born near Baltimore, and came to Winston five years ago. Three years since he started a grocery and confectionery stand at the corner of Fifth and Church streets. Most of our large houses have had their start in small beginnings, and Mr. Huband hopes to increase in stock and patronage.

R. F. GRAHAM.
Fruits and Confectioneries.

R. Frank Graham is a native of Rowan county, and was in mercantile trade at Salisbury for some years. He located in this city in 1882, and has since kept a fruit stand on Fourth street, opposite the courthouse. Tropical and native fruits, confectioneries, tobacco, cigars, etc., are his merchandise.

JONES & WILSON.
Grocery Store.

J. P. Jones of Caswell county and Thos. A. Wilson of this place opened up a neat grocery assortment one door south of Hotel Fountain in April 1888. Their stock speaks for itself.

There are several other small manufacturers, mechanics, dressmakers, meat markets, plenty of saloons, barber shops and small grocery houses, that we have not reached, and there may be other firms of greater importance, and which properly deserve a mention here, that we have inadvertently omitted.

[*Professional, manufacturing, etc., received too late for classification.*]

DR. J. G. ECTOR.
Liberty St. Bet. 6th. and 7th.

Through an inadvertency Dr. Ector's mention was, we regret to say, omitted from the professional pages and as "it is better late than never" we will atone for the oversight by saying that he is a native of Alamance, N. C., attended the Jefferson Medical College of Philadelphia, in 1857, and began practice shortly before the war. Dr. Ector removed to Winston seven years ago and has since been doing his share of practice his residence and office being on Liberty street north of the M. E. church.

G. C. HINE.
Saddle and Harness Manufacturer.

Is a native of this county, and is successor to a business which was established 15 years ago by L. I. Hine, father of the above. In 1880 he purchased the business which, as of yore, is conducted opposite the Starbuck block. Saddles, light and heavy harness and horse goods are carried in stock, or made up to the order of customers, several hands being employed in the trade.

J. W. Shipley, of Baltimore, has for two years past conducted a similar establishment on Main street, near Third.

SPACH & CRANFORD.
Blacksmith and Repair Work.

Edward Spaugh was born in Davidson county, moved to this vicinity in 1841, and ten years later commenced his line of business in Winston. Wm. G. Cranford is from Rowan county, and joined Mr. S. in business two years ago. The firm has recently moved into a new brick shop on Church street, next to Brown's warehouse. General blacksmith work, horse-shoeing, wagon and factory repair work are cared for by this firm. There are several other blacksmiths in the city, but lack of space forbids further mention.

J. H. STOCKTON,
Livery and Sale Stables.

J. H. Stockton was born in Rockingham county reared in Kernersville and in 1861 came to Salem. Four years later he commenced in the trade of Winston, and was one of the firm of Pfohl & Stockton for many years. With this year, Mr. Stockton has opened up a livery barn in rear of Clinard & Brookes' store, where he keeps some twenty animals, several elegant turnouts, and is prepared to accommodate his customers to anything needed in the livery line.

SINGER SEWING MACHINES.
W. B. McWhorter.

The agent for the Singer Manufacturing Company, in Winston, is a native of Lewisburg, W. Va., and came to the management of this office in 1887. The Singer is too well known generally to require any long space from us. Its sales average over a half million of machines each year, which are sent all over the civilized world. The Singer Co. have their principal wood works at South Bend, Ind., and have extensive manufactories of the machinery at Elizabethtown, N. J.; Montreal, Canada; and Glassglow, Scotland.

W. F. BAILY.
Shoe Manufacturer.

Is a native of Davidson county, and commenced the shoe trade twenty years ago having ever since been industriously at the bench. Recently Mr. B. has moved to Winston and his shop is on Liberty street opposite the Gray Block where he is prepared to make any kind of pegged or sewed shoes to the order of customers.

W. E. BECK.
Gun and Locksmith.

Learned his trade with Wm. Dettmar in Salem, worked seven years there, and four years ago started his shop in Winston. His place is on Main street, opposite Brown's warehouse, and Mr. Beck has every requisite for the business.

H. C. McCADDEN'S
Harness Shop.

Near Brown's warehouse on Main street is found the harness shop of H. C. McCadden who has been several years in the business of Winston and turns his principal attention to custom work.

CARE OF THE EYES.
An Important Organ.

Nothing is more important to a man's comfort, happiness, and success in life than good eyesight, and it is every person's duty to take care of these organs. The general health has much to do with the power and endurance of the eyes. Whenever any predisposition to weakness or irritation is shown, late hours and working by artificial light should be studiously avoided, and the eyes bathed frequently in salt and water. On retiring a soft cloth dipped in moderately cold water and partially wrung out, laid upon the eyes and frequently turned over, or redipped, is of great benefit to inflamed eyes.

Many irregularities of sight are found, that need the experience of a skilled optician to accurately fit the proper lens, and we are glad to note that E. Foster Newkirk, at Hotel Fountain, has every necessary appliance for measuring irregularities and making proper adjustments. From personal experience we can fully recommend him

SUMMARY AND REVIEW.

THE FACTS IN A NUT SHELL.
Read This if Nothing More.

In order to give a detailed statement and substantiate our testimony, we have taken up a goodly number of pages in this sketch, and as some of our readers may not have time to carefully go through it *all*, we desire in brief to call your attention to the special features of prominence. In the first eight pages we have presented conclusive evidence that the tide of immigration had turned from the West to the South, and in the salubrity, healthfulness, agricultural and mineral advantages, of this section, given good reasons for our claims of superiority. On several pages we have referred to the fact that manufacturing industries are an essential feature to the permanent prosperity of any city, and we believe that the Chamber of Commerce, as well as the city authorities and our public spirited citizens in general, are impressed with this fact, so that any new enterprise of importance to the place would receive a liberal encouragement. On their behalf whether your line of industry be small or great, if you desire a location in this favored section, we invite you to let us know your needs and wishes and we will make every reasonable effort to accommodate you. The progress of Winston is well illustrated on pages 10–11, showing it to be fifteen times as large to-day as it was 15 years ago. These figures we are prepared to substantiate, and hope to keep a like record for many years to come. Do you desire a city with metropolitan comforts, shaded streets and grassy lawns, at a healthful altitude and with salubrious clime? Come and dwell with us and we will do you good. Our schools, as shown on pages 13–15, are unexcelled, church and society privileges, (pages 16–19), are superb, printing offices and banking accommodations good.

Our manufacturing pages discloses the fact that we have ample conveniences for foundry and repair work.

There are hard woods and valuable timbers in every direction so that nearly any description of wood working industries may be made profitable here. A chair factory with modern styles is especially desirable, spokes, hubs and carriage bent works, and many other kindred industries might be suggested. The cotton and woolen mills so long in successful operation here are a sufficient proof of the feasibility of manufacturing industries in that line. The admirable kaolin, superb pottery clay, fire clay, granite, limestone, etc., of this vicinity, would suggest the propriety of occupations requiring these articles.

Our tobacco interests, which give employment to 5,000 persons, have been fully written upon, (pages 31–44), and comprise a leading feature of the place. This is fully represented with the exception perhaps of snuff mills and cigarette factories, which might each find here the material and facilities for successful operation.

Under mercantile interests, page 70, we gave figures illustrating the magnitude of the dried fruit product of this section. As the lands of Western North Carolina seem to possess the property of imparting a peculiarly fine flavor not only to tobacco, but to large and small fruits, there is every reason why a canning factory of mammoth proportions might be made a profitable investment in this place. We have before made mention, page 11, of the lands of Forsyth county, but we especially desire to emphasize the fact that, *it has already been clearly demonstrated that the soil of this section has a peculiar tenacity in the retention of fertilizers, and that however poor the land may appear to be, it is easily revived and put in condition to bring forth an abundant harvest.* The apparently poor sections are found to be perfectly adapted to the growth of all kinds of fruits and berries, the natural home of the grape, raising the finest wine producing vines to be found in the States. No better section of the world can be found for common or high bred poultry, and its never failing streams, with abundance of nutritious grasses, and healthful atmosphere, gives to Western N. C. as fine a country as the far famed "Blue Grass Region" of Kentucky, in which to breed blooded cattle and horses. There are several small herds of Jerseys in this county, a stud or two of Hambletonian horses, but these industries are yet in their infancy and present a splendid field for investment.

On other pages we have called attention to the minerals of this region, coal, iron, etcetera, which will doubtless be developed with the advent of coming railroads. North Carolina has proven to be one of the richest mineral States in the Union, embracing besides all sorts of building stones, and the coarser minerals before mentioned, gold and gems of rare beauty. There are beryls, aquamarines, garnets and amethysts. Mica is found in great abundance and in the largest plates known. It is a substantiated fact that Winston-Salem is a progressive place, and that we have more manufacturing machinery in operation than any other city of the State.

The Twin-City is in great need of a well operated street car line, and will doubtless soon have a company formed for that purpose. As remarked elsewhere a fashionable hotel, or a well conducted sanitarium near the mineral spring, would prove good investments.

Finally, let us add, if you have no desire to enter the field for manufacture or agriculture, and are perchance seeking for a health resort for yourself or some member of your family, prostrated with nervous troubles, or debilitated with lung or throat affections, which need a bracing and health-giving atmosphere, protected from the northern blizzards by the Blue Ridge mountains, give this city or county a trial and we are certain you will remain with us. The Chamber of Commerce, City Officials or the business men mentioned in these pages, will doubtless be glad to answer any reasonable questions, on subjects in their particular line, and to them we refer you for special information.

The South will never realize its full measure of greatness and prosperity until it is more densely populated, and although our resources are superb and our natural advantages almost illimitable, still the measure of our prosperity is the measure of our ability to develop those resources. It is just as well, therefore, that intelligent and industrious men from other sections of the country should be invited to come among us and aid us in the work of development. And this invitation should be based upon a truthful presentation of the facts, and not founded upon those gorgeous exaggerations which read like circus posters and which have unquestionably hurt the cause of immigration elsewhere, and perhaps to some extent in the South.

Some features of interest we have yet failed to mention. The museum of Antiquities, in connection with the Salem Boys' School, is worthy of notice, the Southern Express here is conducted by Mayor Buford.

Since compiling our school pages Jas. A. Gray has taken the place of Col. Gorrell on the Board. The name of Rev. C. H. Wiley, who was early in the school movement and Chairman of the first Board, was inadvertently omitted. Prof. W. A. Blair has been elected Superintendent.

In mention of the organization of the Forsyth Riflemen, the reader might infer that the present officers were its organizers, while our worthy postmaster S. H. Smith, was a prime mover and the first Captain.

KERNERSVILLE.

FORSYTH COUNTY'S SECOND TOWN.

Its Progress, Business Interests, Advantages and Surroundings.

KERNERSVILLE.

FORSYTH COUNTY'S SECOND TOWN.
Its Progress, Business Interests, Advantages and Surroundings.

How many hundreds of people in the northern tier of these United States, who suffer from the weekly recurrence of frigid waves, for six months of the year, sometimes coming with such intensity as to freeze the mercury and ruin constitutions of natural vigor, would gladly accept the manifold advantages of this favored clime if they but knew them? How to convey the real facts without exaggeration, in a shape to be preserved for months and years by those who are its fortunate recipients, has been the study and aim of the compiler and projectors of this pamphlet. Perhaps no handsomer site could have been found in the State for a pleasant village than the location of Kernersville, and, of its history and surroundings we shall proceed to write.

About the year 1760 this nearly level plateau, upon the county's water shed, was selected by Caleb Story, an Irishman, who, it is said bought 400 acres for four gallons of rum. A few years later Story sold his interest to a Mr. Dobson, the place for many years being know as Dobson's Cross Roads. Rev. Gotlieb Sholer, of Salem, purchased this homestead in 1806 for his son Nathaniel and the Sholers sold to Joseph Kerner in 1817, from whom the place takes its name. Mr. Kerner was born in Germany in 1768, came to America in 1782, bringing with him an illustration of Christ Before Pontius Pilate, which had been sketched from a stone engraving, found under an ancient church at Vienna, a reproduction of which is still preserved in many of the Kernersville homes. He was in agricultural pursuits near Friedland before removing to this place in 1818,

and at his death in 1830 he owned about 1,100 acres around these corners, which fell to his heirs, John F. Philip and Salome. The daughter married Appolis Harmon, of Connecticut. Mr. Harmon died in 1844, leaving his interest to his sons, Rufus and Julius who have spent their lives here as millwrights, farmers or in carpentering.

John Frederick Kerner raised a family of six sons and three daughters, all still living.

Phillip Kerner has five living children. J. G. is an artist of rare ability whose unique house on Main street, erected at a cost of about $5,000, has excited much comment. It is a square brick, with Gothic roof, and combines parlors, dining-room, kitchen, ball-room, bed-rooms, furnaces, Dutch-oven, smoke-house, wood-house, wagon-house, hay-loft and horse-stalls all under one roof. It comes from the ideas of genius, and its ceilings and walls are elaborately decorated with rare designs of ornamental painting, which would grace the costliest mansion in the land.

Kernersville was a quiet country hamlet of about 100 inhabitants in 1870, but railroad matters began to be talked of, and the place was incorporated in 1872, including an area of 1½ mile in diameter, with the academy building as the central point, and in this territory were found 147 inhabitants. The citizens donated, almost too liberally, and graded four miles of the railroad, which reached here in 1873. The census of 1880 showed about 500 inhabitants, and the estimate of to-day places the population fully double these figures, thus showing it to be progressive. There are more brick residences, stores and factories, in Kernersville, than any other town of its size in the State, thus showing it to be substantial. This is an excellent brick clay, and the dirt from the cellar is often used at once to make the brick for the superstructure.

The plateau upon which the village is built excites the admiration of all who consider its features. Not in any sense mountainous, it is the watershed of this region, having perhaps the highest altitude of any non-mountainous point in the State. It lies 1100 feet above the sea, 150 feet higher than Greensboro, 70 above High Point, 50 feet higher than Forsyth Court-house, and about the same above Mt. Airy depot. On this eminence, Pilot and Sauratown mountains, 30 miles to the northwest, can be plainly seen, and the Blue Ridge Ridge peaks on a clear day are discernable as a misty veil in the dim distance. From this place the waters flow in all directions, the rivulets going to assist in forming Belew's Creek, Abbott's Creek, Muddy Creek, Reedy Fork, Haw River and Deep River, thus giving a natural drainage and insuring a salubrity and healthgiving atmosphere. The winds for a few days in Winter are quite bleak, but so mild and tame when compared with a northern or western blizzard as to almost be called spring-like. The unobstructed elevation gives a pleasant breeze for the hottest day in summer, and insures refreshing sleep for the night.

CHURCHES, SCHOOLS, ETC.

The Kerners and early settlers here were Moravians, a brief history of whom we gave on pages 9, 15–16, illustrating their traits of integrity and persevering industry, and this was a place for occasional preaching early in this century. Rev. C. L. Rights, the present Presiding Elder of the Southern Province of the Moravian Church, preached his first sermon here in 1846. He was born in Salem, in 1820, served a printer's apprentice in Greensboro, and at Salisbury, worked in Blum's printing house several years before entering the ministry. The Kernersville Moravians had their church house at Freidland until 1867, when the present neat brick structure was erected in this place, largely by the generosity of Dr. E. Kerner. Rev. Rights came to this charge 16 years ago, and has been a faithful spiritual shepherd.

The M. E. Church South, erected a comfortable brick structure here in 1877 to take the place of the old frame structure which had been built here in about 1840.

The Baptist Organization were fortunate in having the philanthropic Mrs. Alonzo Brown in their midst, and her efforts brought forth a commodious brick house of worship in 1886.

The Methodist Protestants erected their brick edifice last year, were generously assisted by J. C. Roberts, and have a good place for worship.

The Presbyterians have an organization, but as yet no spiritual home. They have the privilege of the Moravian church when occasion requires.

There is a colored A. M. E. and Baptist church, both having houses for worship.

The public schools of the State are accomplishing much good and those of this place are flourishing under the principalship of Rev. J. W. Pinnix a native of Caswell county, who has been teacher and preacher for a dozen years past and came to the charge of our schools four years ago. The enrollment at the last term was over 100, and Mr. Rush of the colored free schools had nearly as many under his charge. Prof. Pinnix is assisted by Misses Mary McKaughan and Lucy Perry. He has charge over christian churches in Randolph and Guilford counties.

A private school has been conducted by Mrs. C. L. Rights, in the Moravian vestry, with good success for ten years past. The Academy was built by a stock company in 1859, and has for the past ten years been run under auspices of this Conference of the M. E. Church South. Prof. H.

L. Coble, from Randolph county, the newly elected Principal, will take charge this month. He comes highly recommended, and will endeavor to put the school on an elevated plane, so that Kernersville will offer not only one of the sightliest, healthiest and most pleasant locations in the State, but high educational, moral and social advantages.

Prof. John S. Ray is Chairman of the County Board of Education, has achieved a literary standing worthy of record. He came to the charge of our Academy in 1870, and was teacher here for several years.

MAYORS, ETC.—The venerable Joseph Armfield, born May 6, 1800, was first Mayor of this place, and was succeeded by Dr. A. D. Lindsay, who, after his third election, retired in favor of Prof. J. S. Ray, who held the position for several terms. A. H. S. Beard, Dr. E. Kerner, J. C. Roberts, J. N. Guyer and L. E. Griffith have served the incorporation. Mayor L. F. Davis, the present incumbent, is a native of Guilford county, and for three years past in mercantile trade here, under which heading he will have further notice.

COMMISSIONERS, ETC.—J. M. Greenfield, J. H. Hester, J. S. King, J. N. Leak and W. A. Lowrey, all enterprising business men of the place, serve as Commissioners, Mr. Lowrey officiating as Secretary and Treasurer. W. A. Linville is town police, I. H. McKaughn is deputy sheriff and tax collector.

The Trustees to the Academy are Dr. B. J. Sapp, J. F. Plunkett, W. A. Lowrey, R. P. Kerner, W. A Griffith.

The School Commissioners are I. H. McKaughan, Henry Perry and Pinkney Ballard.

THE POST-OFFICE at this place has recently been given to DeWitt Harmon, by request of J. H. Lindsay, who has just resigned, on account of an appointment as a teacher at the Staunton Deaf and Dumb Institute in Virginia. Mr. Harmon is a native of the place, educated at our academy and taught school at Nazareth, Pa., for two terms, having since been salesman for Beard & Roberts. This place was a mail crossing at an early date, and Joseph Kerner, his sons, Phillip and John F., Lucinda Kerner, John H. Hester, John King, Jos. E. Kerner, have held the office prior to Mr. Lindsay. The receipts of the office are about $500 per year. There are two daily mails each way by rail, and a daily mail to and from Summerfield, 12 miles to the northward.

RAILROAD EXPRESS, ETC.—The Kernersville station was first in charge of C. B. Brooks, of Salem, held for a short time by F. G. Shifent, who resigned November, 1873, and Richard P. Kerner, the present agent, took charge December 1st, of that year. He was teacher and in farming pursuits here before accepting the railroad business. In addition to general freight and passenger traffic, the agent here also has charge of the Southern express and Western Union telegraph trade, being assisted in these matters, especially telegraphy, by his son, John G. Fresh fruits by express, manufactured tobacco, granite and dried fruits by freights are the principal shipments. White oak timber for switch ties and bridge timber is also a valuable product of the place.

The Kernersville News was started by T. A. Lyon and H. C. Edwards, Apr. 1st '81 as a 5 col. folio afterwards enlarged to a 6 col. folio and finally to 7 columns. It was at first printed on a small hand press. It was bought by J. H. Lindsay July 1st 1883 and all the old type has been replaced by new—also new cases, stands and jobbing outfit added. A year ago by the aid of citizens, he secured a Campbell Power Press, to prevent his accepting a position elsewhere. There are printed at this office besides the *News*, the Thomasville

Gazette and the Summerfield *Gleaner*. The job patronage has largely increased and it has become one of the best paying country papers in North Carolina. J. H. Lindsay has been unanimously re-elected Sec'y and Treas. of the N. C. Press Association three times in succession. He has been untiring in his zeal for the upbuilding of this place, but having been offered a lucrative position at Staunton, Va., will go there in a few days and leaves the field open here, for a good newspaper man.

HOTELS, PHYSICIANS, ETC.

Dr. B. J. Sapp was born and reared in Guilford county, three miles east of this place, attended Rush Medical College at Chicago, 1859-60, practiced in the army, and in 1867 began in the profession here, opening a boarding house on Depot street in connection with his practice, and in 1880 purchased the old Kernersville hotel stand, which has been a place of public entertainment for nearly 100 years. The doctor has good accommodations, and keeps the only regular hotel of the place. In 1874-5 Dr. Sapp attended medical lectures in Baltimore, and graduated from the Washington University (now College of Physicians and Surgeons). Dr. Sapp has been the principal druggist of this place for many years past, keeping quite a full stock of medicines, chemicals and sundries, which he runs in connection with the hotel trade, and also does a fair share of practice. He is assisted in the business by his son, Luther L., who is reading, preparatory to entering medical college. Carey C. Sapp, the doctor's oldest son, graduated from the Baltimore Dental College last year, and is practicing at Statesville.

Mr. *Israel Kerner* was born in this vicinity in 1821, and has kept a public house nearly all his life, six years ago swinging out the hotel sign at the "Y" on Main street. The house is a brick structure, with about a dozen rooms, and its proprietor the oldest Kerner living in this county.

Dr. *Elias Kerner* was born in this place in 1826, attended the medical department of the Pennsylvania University at Philadelphia in 1849, practiced a year in Salem with the late Dr. Zeveley, and has since been dispensing pills and powders in this place and surrounding country. In 1859 he built his fine brick residence on Main street, and in 1876 assisted his father in the erection of the saw and grist mill a mile west of town, which is now owned by himself and son, R. B., the flourishing Winston attorney.

Dr. *A. D. Lindsay* is a native of Guilford county, attended lectures at the University of Pennsylvania in 1850-1, having practiced in this place and surrounding vicinity ever since, excepting two years which he spent at Hickory Tavern, and a time as post surgeon in the late war.

Dr. *L. I. Bodenhamer* is a native of Davidson county, and for fourteen years a resident of Kernersville. He has been a preacher in the Primitive Baptist Church for thirty-five years past, having for many years had charge of the "Saints' Delight" congregation, six miles west of town. For twenty-five years past Dr. Bodenhamer has done some practice, and more recently has given it his entire attention, last winter taking a course of lectures at the College of Physicians and Surgeons of Baltimore, Md.

Dr. *W. P. Dix* is a native of Randolph county, began mercantile trade here some twenty-five years ago. Later, after a preparatory course, he engaged in practice at Walkertown, where he practiced for twenty years, in the meantime graduating from the Baltimore Medical college in 1874, and removing to this place about three years ago.

ATTRACTIVE FEATURES.

From Madison, near the Dan river, to Salisbury, on the Yadkin, a distance of nearly sixty miles, is found a ridge, or water shed, dividing Western North Carolina from that portion farther east, and, although living streams are found on all sides, this ridge can be traversed the whole distance without crossing the water. About midway on this elevation, 11 miles east of Winston, in Forsyth county, and 18 miles west of Greensboro, is found the hadsome site of Kernersville. The main street is hadsomely shaded, and adorned with many brick residences, stores and factories. Roads center here from eight directions, giving easy access to the surrounding agricultural, fruit and tobacco lands. It is perhaps unexcelled as a general fruit raising section, and Forsyth and adjoining counties, as shown on page 31, abound with excellent tobacco lands of which none are superior to this ridge. What we have said on page 83 regarding the raising of fine stock, nutritious grasses and abundance of the best water in the world, is applicable in ever sense to this section. Springs come forth from nearly every hillside, and wells of the purest water can be tapped at a few feet below the surface.

This place is in need of a bank to accommodate the monied interest of our merchants and manufacturers, and some enterprising man would do well to invest a few thousand dollars in that direction.

Mr. J. W. Beard, one of the largest real estate and business dealers here, offers handsome sites for manufacturing, adjacent to the railroad, free to any one who will erect substantial factories. He will also give free residence lots to any person who will build a good dwelling house. Mr. Beard owns a quarry of superb granite, only a quarter of a mile from the depot, which he will sell or lease on easy terms to parties desiring to develop the same.

BUSINESS INTERESTS.

What has been said of the tobacco interests on page 31 has a direct bearing upon the surroundings of of this place, as some of the best tobacco lands in the country are found in this vicinity. Kernersville also has two warehouses and five manufactories, which will be mentioned in detail.

The outcrop of granite in this vicinity is superb, and the sample monument, near our depot, with many tons that have been shipped, are the best of testimony as to its superior quality and capacity for splendid finish. Unlimited quarries are found here in close proximity to the depot, and present a fine field for development.

What we have said on page 70 regarding dried fruits and their flavor is particularly applicable to this section, as the surrounding hills and dales are perfectly adapted to abundant fruit crops of the finest flavor; hence this place would make a favorable site for a canning factory, and the citizens offer liberal inducements towards the establishment of any enterprise of that kind.

Numerous liberal offers are given to actual settlers for residence or business sites, and persons will be welcomed from any section of the country.

BEARD & ROBERTS,

Tobacco Man'fr's and General Store.

While we cannot go into lengthy detail in private matters, yet to give some idea of the business of the village, it is only proper that several of the leading firms here should be fairly represented and among the most prominent, both in mercantile and manufacturing transactions here, the above firm deserves to be classed.

J. W. Beard is a native of Davidson county, serving for several years as a salesman for a New York clothing house. He commenced business here with his brother in charge, in 1866, a half dozen years later investing largely in the real estate of the place, building his elegant brick residence in 1873 and a year later accepting J. C. Roberts as a partner in trade. The firm erected their large two-story brick store in 1879. This is 26x112 feet and filled with a very complete assortment in all lines of general merchandise, comprising dry-goods, clothing, boots and shoes, hats, groceries and grocer's drugs, hardware, notions, house furnishing and everything properly coming under this general heading. The firm deal largely in country produce, dried fruits and berries for shipments. Their tobacco business was begun in 1880, and the factory was erected in 1884, and adds largely to the business aspect of the village in the vicinity of the depot. It is of brick, 52x136 feet and having five floors, its capacity would be nearly half a million pounds. The annual output has been from 100,000 to 150,000, requiring the services of 50 to 75 hands in its production. The trade as with other dealers is largely in the South and "Beard's Favorite" is widely known among dealers. "Sweet Relief," "Piedmont Beauty," "Old Gold," and several other popular brands are on their old list and with the present year they have started a new brand called "Red Devon," which is designed as a superior chew.

Messrs. Beard & Roberts are both men of push and enterprise, of liberal business dealings, largely interested in real estate and ever ready to do a fair share towards any enterprise for the promotion of the place.

W. H. LEAK & CO.,
Plug and Twist Tobacco.

W. H. & J. N. Leak are natives of Guilford county, the former having been engaged in the manufacture of tobacco in Stokes county for several years prior to opening the first factory here, in 1873. The enterprise was run by W. H. Leak until 1880, when B. A. Brown and N. W. Sapp were accepted as partners under firm style of W. H. Leak & Co. J. N. Leak was an assistant in the early part of the business here but subsequently was in merchandising at Lexington for 5 years and returning here in 1882 he purchased N. W. Sapp's interest in the factory. Two years later the Leak Brothers bought out Mr. Brown's interest continuing the old firm style of W. H. Leak & Co. Employment is given to 50 or 60 hands and the annual output is about 100,000 pounds of fine grade tobacco which is sold to wholesale jobbers. W. H. Leak has charge of the leaf purchases and his long experience has made him an expert in that line. J. N. looks after office matters and all departments of the trade are under careful supervision. A leading specialty in brands is "Leak's Best," 12 inch 3's and "Cock of the Walk," (Broad Gauge) 10 in. 4's.

BROWN, SAPP & CO.,
Tobacco Manufacturers.

As mentioned under a former notice B. A. Brown and N. W. Sapp were formerly in the tobacco manufacture in company with W. H. Leak. Having retired from that firm they in 1884 in company with J. Van Lindley, of the Pomona Hill nurseries, near Greensboro, built the large brick factory near the depot and opened up manufacture in that line. The structure is 40x90 three stories in height and with rear addition of 40x16 feet. The firm work 50 or 60 hands turning out about 100,000 pounds annually. Among their standard brands are, Good News, Jenny Lind, Tube Rose, Knights of Labor and others. Institutions of this kind are important factors in the prosperity of the place.

Do not destroy this book, as you will want to refer to it again.

J. M. GREENFIELD,
Plug and Twist Tobacco.

J. M. Greenfield, a native of Lexington, N. C., joined T. E. Kerner, (who died a year since) seven years ago in the manufacture of tobacco, and a couple of years since the firm erected the three-story brick, 40x80, which is a handsome addition to the many brick structures on West Main street. The dirt excavated for the basement was made into brick and used for the superstructure, and that plan set the ball to rolling for continued development of a similar nature. Mr. Greenfield's trade is principally in the Carolinas and Georgia, and some of his leading brands are "Success," "Reform," "New Era," "Free Trade," and many others. He is an enterprising business man, works a goodly number of hands, and the aggregate of his disbursements for tobacco leaf and wages amounts to many thousands annually.

LOWREY & STAFFORD.
Tobacco Manufacturers.

Born in this village, W. A. Lowrey was reared in agricultural pursuits in the country, but a few years since, to give his children the advantages of education which this place affords, he moved to town and engaged in manufacturing with E. J. Stafford, his son-in-law. Mr. Stafford is also a native of the place, was book-keeper at Tatum, S. C., for ten years, and returned to this place January, 1886. The partners both give strict personal attention to the details of manufacture, and produce desirable goods. The members of the firm have both bought real estate in the village, and at no distant day expect to erect a brick factory.

Mercantile Interests.

Many years ago the dried fruit shipping interest of this section was a prominent feature, and it still continues to be a factor in trade, but as express lines have brought us so near the great markets, many bushels of peaches, berries, cherries and the like are now sent fresh to the cities, thus, to some extent, making dried fruits of secondary importance. There are always large quantities of products that get too ripe before plucking, are slightly damaged, or otherwise inferior for shipment, thus illustrating that a canning factory is an institution greatly to be desired here, and if some one who understands the business will engage in the enterprise, they will be liberally seconded by the citizens of this place. Almost any product, excepting tropical fruits, will thrive on these hills, or in the fertile valleys. Fruit evaporators have been run here for several years past with good success, having been introduced in 1883 by Mr. Hatch, of New York, and two years later nine evaporators were in use in the village.

L. F. DAVIS & SON.
General Merchandise.

L. F. Davis was raised in agricultural pursuits, and ten years since commenced merchandising at Deep River, in Guilford county. Three years ago he moved to this place, bought real estate, built his present store building, and in company with his son, E. Grant, conducts a general merchandise store, keeping the usual requisites of stores in that line. The firm is located near the depot, and in three years of trade have secured a fair share of the business. Mr. Davis owns several lots in the village on which he will give bargains to actual settlers, and a mile south of town he has a 70-acre farm, which he offers on easy terms, as he does not care to again engage in farming.

N. W. SAPP.
General Merchandise.

Guilford county line comes within one mile and a half of this village, and N. W. Sapp was born three miles from here in that county. He was clerking in the place for Mr. Hester prior to the war, and after the close of hostilities continued with his old employer for a time, but in 1869 opened up trade for himself, and has since been at the oldest grocery corner of the place. Mr. Sapp keeps a well assorted stock of general merchandise, and his many years in trade has given him a wide acquaintance. Seven years ago he engaged in manufacturing with W. H. Leak, later becoming one of the firm of Brown, Sapp & Co., mentioned elsewhere. Mr. Sapp is one of the county commissioners, having been re-elected in June.

B. A. BROWN & CO.,
General Merchandise.

B. A. Brown is a native of Guilford county, and in 1880 engaged in tobacco manufacturing here, later becoming the senior partner of Brown, Sapp & Co., tobacconists. D. A. Bodenhamer is from Davidson county, and for several years was in the livery business here. About Christmas last the firm opened up a large stock of general merchandise, keep a full stock of dry goods, groceries, clothing, hats, shoes, and the usual requirements of family supplies. Their quick appreciation of the public wants and readiness to supply them has brought them a large share of trade.

J. S. KING,
Grocery and Provision Store.

J. S. King, like many other business men of this place, was born in Guilford county, and began clerking for his brother at his present corner fourteen years ago. In 1879 John L. King built the handsome brick corner where the business is now conducted, and three years later the present proprietor purchased the stock which he has since replenished from time to time with all the requirements of a general grocery and provision store. Mr. King also keeps a stock of boots and shoes.

KERNER & CO.,

At the Main street "Y," adjoining the old Kerner House, a stock of groceries, confections and fruits was opened out in May by 3 young men of the village name. O. W. Kerner is the industrious bookkeeper at Vaughn & Pepper's wholesale and retail house, Winston; J. F. is operator at this station, and the management of the stock is in charge of J. G., the junior partner.

APPLE & HUNT,
Milliners and Mantua Makers.

The milliner's trade and making of ladies' wearing apparel are necessary adjuncts to our social features, and Miss Mary Apple, of Reidsville, has been for several years in the trade. Mrs. C. W. Hunt, of this village, was formerly in the trade, and the twain last year opened up a good stock of millinery, keeping also notions, fancy goods and a few dress patterns.

J. W. CREWS,
Flour, Feed and Guano.

Artificial fertilizers have become an important feature in the agricultural productions of all sections of the country, and the farmers here on the lighter grade of upland soil fully appreciate its value. Mr. Crews sells the Navassa guano.

R. A. DUGGINS,
Barber Shop.

Here is another business unclassified, but essential to comfort, and supplied in this place by R. A. Duggins, a native of the village, who has been thirteen years in the business, and last year built a convenient shop near the depot.

R. A. JORDAN,
Livery Stable.

This business comes neither under merchadise or manufacturing, but is yet important to any progressive village. R. A. Jordan is a native of the place, and owns quite a large number of lots in the village, which can be bought for improvement at low figures. He has been for nine years past in the livery business, and keeps all kinds of stock and turnouts necessary for the accommodation of the people who desire livery hire.

MISCELLANEOUS MANUFACTURING.

The permanency of any place is greatly enhanced by miscellaneous manufacturing. Even though they be but small, and employing but few hands, they open a field for development and give values to raw materials. There are a number of fields in which miscellaneous manufacturing appears to hold out inducements here. Living is cheap and laborers plenty, and this village, as all other enterprising towns in the south, will give capitalists a hearty welcome.

HUFF & STUART.
Carriage Manufacturing.

F. K. Huff is a native of this county, and has had over a dozen of years experience as a carriage upholster, trimmer and painter. He was for five years a partner with Mr. Lewis, as Lewis & Huff, and a year since, in company with J. R. Stuart of Forsyth, county he opened up trade south of the depot. The firm erected a neat two story building, equipped with elevator and modern requisites, where they are prepared to turn out all kinds of custom work in the most approved manner. Mr. Stuart has had nine years experience as a blacksmith and superintends that department which is conducted in a detached building near the factory. Many of his well-wrought hammers and other tools are of his own manufacture evincing genius at the forge. The new firm are prepared to do good work and will spare no effort to meet the requirements of trade.

A. LEWIS.
Carriage Manufacturer.

Mr. A. Lewis is a native of Davie county this State and commenced the carriage business in 1857 opening up a shop in this village where he has now been industriously engaged in turning out vehicles for 31 years. Several hundreds have went forth from his establishment and his buggies and carriages can be found in many barns of this and adjoining counties. He has disbursed for wages and material a large amount of money in this place.

Wagon Making.—W. H. Harrell, a native of Guilford county, with thirty years experience has been for four years past in the wagon trade here.

Blacksmithing is closely allied to wagon making, and this village has two smiths.

The Saw-Mill is the property of H. C. Edwards, has steam fixtures and does good work.

Harness, Saddles, Etc., have become in this town identified with the name of Haley Davis, who is a native of the county, commenced the business in 1845, and a year later moved to this place, where he has since industriously followed his occupation.

A Tannery has been run by Nathaniel M. Kerner for many years, and is still in successful operation.

Shoe Making and repairing is conducted by L. B. Hester, a native of this vicinity, who has been in the trade for eight years past.

In order to compare our climate with that of the North, we append the following weather record, taken from a journal published in northwestern Pennsylvania: No. of rainy days, 193; snowy days, 81; fair days, 191. January 8th was the coldest day of the year, mercury falling 24 degrees below zero. July 7th was the warmest day of the year, mercury rising to 103 degrees above. Extremes of cold and heat, 127 degrees. January had the greatest number of days in which snow fell, there being 23. October had 14 rainy days, while July and August were equal in the number of fair days, each having 24; rain fell on 7 days each of the last named months, but rather light.

OAK RIDGE INSTITUTE.

In writing up Winston-Salem, a brief outlook into the industries and institutions of the surrounding country may not be uninteresting. Taking the Salisbury and Danville road from Kernersville toward the north-east, six miles drive through one of the finest wheat and fruit growing section of Piedmont, N. C. brings us in view of one of the finest High Schools of the South, Oak Ridge Institute. We say one of the finest, and we mean what we say, for it may justly be so termed, by its reputation for honest, conscientious, thorough work, by its first-class buildings and equipments, by its large roll, comprising for the past year 219 names, representing six states and two territories, and by the prominent positions its students are taking and holding in the actual every day business affairs of the Country—This school has been owned and operated by Profs. J. A. and M. H. Holt as principals for over ten years and assisted by an efficient and experienced corps of teachers. These young men are native North Carolinians, and have learned by years of practical experience what the needs of the South are, and they have accordingly arranged, not only a practical and complete Literary course of study, fitting its possessors for college or for life, but a Business College course as well, equal to the best North or South, whose graduates hold honored positions in various towns of the South. For beauty and healthfulness of situation, Oak Ridge Institute cannot be surpassed. Her beautiful groves of native oak, her elegant Christian culture, and to crown all, her cherished Institution lifting its classic proportions grandly above the Oaks about it, altogether leave upon the memory a grand picture. To be appreciated Oak Ridge and Oak Ridge Institute must be seen and patronized. Herewith we present you with a cut of the Institue. Those wishing information about the Institute or surrounding country should

Address, Profs. J. A. and M. H. Holt, Oak Ridge, N. C.

SENTINEL JOB OFFICE.
Fitted in First-Class Order.

The Sentinel job office has always been the largest in the Twin City, and recently it has been put in good shape. Modern and beautiful faces of job type, the largest paper cutter in the city, and other improvements have been added, and skilled workmen, with years of experience in job work, have accepted positions with us. We are now turning out as handsome printing as is done in the State, and our prices are as low as is consistent with first-class work. School and catalogue printing and office stationery are our specialties. Send in a trial order. We guarantee satisfaction.

JOB PRINTING OFFICE.
At Orlando Florida.

I have a new job office for sale at a great sacrifice, for cash or on easy terms. The office cost about $2,000, has a first-class cutter, two elegant jobbers, 500 pounds of body type, thirty to thirty-five fonts of job type, metal furniture, and everything practical. Orlando is the progressive city of South Florida, and Orange, the banner county of the State. Good reasons given for selling.

Address,   D. P. ROBBINS,
Erie, Pa., or Orlando, Fla.

FLORIDA LANDS.
Town Lots or Grove Tracts.

Having secured through advertising, and various trading, town lots and tracts for grove purposes in a half dozen different counties of Florida, I have bargains to offer to any one wishing property in the orange State. I have spent two years in the State, and have selected my purchases in the most desirable portion of the peninsula, viz., Orange, Lake, Sumter, Pasco, Hernando and Polk counties. I have town lots worth from $15 to $200 each, orange lands $10 to 50 per acre.

To those desiring information about Florida or the preservation of health, my published book on Health, Happiness, Hygiene, and Florida, is worth many times its cost. Well bound, 800 octavo pages, sent postpaid for $2.50.

Address, D. P. ROBBINS, M. D.,
Erie, Penn'a.

OUR REGARDS.
Valedictory.

The writer of this special edition cannot close without extending to the business men and citizens of this section in general his sincere thanks for their very cordial reception of this enterprise, and the generous assistance which they have rendered in the work. Our duties have been arduous, but were made very much lighter by the kind reception with which we have been met by Forsyth county hospitality, and while our work is necessarily imperfect in many particulars, we hope it will not be unworthy of the wide distribution which its friends have already guaranteed, and that it will redound to the future good of this section. We have made very many pleasant acquaintances, and wherever our lot may be cast in the future, we shall always have a kind remembrance of the unselfish interest displayed toward the Descriptive Sketch of Winston-Salem, which is a sufficient guarantee that any legitimate enterprise will have the generous encouragement of the good people of this city. Success to the tobacco city of North Carolina with all her enterprises, and may her natural wealth, beautiful surroundings and generosity be fully appreciated!

Every year the South is becoming more popular as a place for health, comfort, and business.

The older this book becomes, the more valuable it will be for reference.

[*Winston matter received too late for classification.*]

Contractors and Mechanics.

J. C. MILLER,
Carpenter and Builder.

Was born on the west side of Winston, assisted in grubbing the court-house square, and has lived in the city since it was made the county seat. Mr. Miller has helped to build a large majority of the business blocks, factories and residences of the new city, having been foreman of outside work for Miller Bros. 15 years, and for two years past in contract work for himself. He has a planer and wood-working shop on North Liberty street.

W. F. KEITH

Is a native of Raleigh, and has been a plasterer for 16 years. He came to this place in 1875, and has done his full share of service in both plain and ornamental designs, and has given full satisfaction as a mechanic.

A. J. GALE

Is a native of Bristol, England, and has been in this city for a dozen years. He is a contractor and brick mason, and was one of the prominent workers on the M. E. Church graded school building and a score of other business blocks.

North Carolina has an area of territory about as large as England, and within her borders are resources such as the latter country never knew. Her rivers and streams abound with fish of almost every known description and unequaled for food. Her forests contain all sorts of game, besides timber in almost inexhaustible abundance, of the most valuable sorts, and in the bowels of her earth are mines of untold wealth, such as the world has never dreamed of, and which science will bring to the surface and pour into the waiting and willing lap of commerce.

From the great difficulty in securing the concluding facts in any department under consideration we have failed to make the arrangement as systematic as would have been desirable, but by consulting the table of contents on inside cover page any article may readily be found.

WEBSTER'S UNABRIDGED.
STANDARD AND BEST.

3000 more Words and nearly **2000** more Illustrations than any other American Dictionary.

Among the supplementary features, original with **Webster's Unabridged** and unequaled for concise and trustworthy information, are

A Biographical Dictionary

Containing nearly 10,000 names of Noteworthy Persons, with their nationality, station, profession or occupation, date of birth and death, (if deceased), etc.,

A Gazetteer of the World

Of over 25,000 Titles, locating and briefly describing the Countries, Cities, Towns, and Natural Features of every part of the Globe, and The Explanatory and Pronouncing Vocabulary of the names of

Noted Fictitious Persons

and Places, such as are often referred to in literature and conversation. The latter is not found in any other Dictionary.

WEBSTER IS THE STANDARD

Authority in the Gov't Printing Office, and with the **U. S. Supreme Court.** It is recommended by the **State Sup'ts of Schools of 36 States**, and by leading **College Pres'ts** of U. S. and Canada. It is the only Dictionary that has been selected in making **State Purchases** for Schools, and nearly all the **School Books** are based upon it.

An invaluable companion in every School and at every Fireside. Specimen pages and testimonials sent prepaid on application.
Published by **G. & C. MERRIAM & CO.,**
Springfield, Mass., U. S. A.

-:- CHAMBER OF COMMERCE -:-
—OF—
Winston-Salem, N. C.

THIS organization was founded in 1885, its objects being to advance the mercantile and manufacturing interests of Winston and Salem, to promote internal improvements, encourage immigration, collect and distribute information to the interests of our cities, and to discuss and regulate commercial usages, adjust differences and disputes in trade.

In order to diffuse general information regarding this place and the surrounding country, its features and advantages, this pamphlet has been compiled under auspices of a committee from our body and its general information has been carefully supervised to prevent exaggerations or misstatements.

The compiler has been very conservative in his statements, and the general advantages have not been overdrawn.

Persons desiring special information about this section of country, with the view of locating here, will be cheerfully responded to by addressing the CHAMBER OF COMMERCE, Winston, N. C.

The following list of names of the officers and committees comprise many of the most influential business men of the Twin-City:

OFFICERS:

J. C. BUXTON, *Pres.*   J. W. FRIES, *First Vice-Pres.*   W. A. WHITAKER, *Second Vice-Pres.*
J. D. PAYLOR, *Secretary and Treasurer.*

DIRECTORS:

R. D. BROWN,   H. E. FRIES,   R. J. REYNOLDS,   C. A. FOGLE,   JNO. W. HANES,
C. A. HEGE,   JAS. A. GRAY.

ARBITRATION COMMITTEE:

C. HAMLEN,   T. J. BROWN,   C. H. FOGLE,   P. H. HANES.

COMMITTEES

of the Chamber of Commere to serve from Oct. 1st, 1887 to Oct. 1st, 1888.

On Information, Statistics, Telegraphing and Letters,
W. A. WHITAKER,   J. W. FRIES,   TAYLOR BYNUM,   A. B. GORRELL,
C. A. HEGE.

On Trade and Transportation.
J. W. HANES,   J. E. GILMER,   J. M. ROGERS,   F. H. FRIES.

On Internal Improvements and Immigration.
G. W. HINSHAW,   C. B. WATSON,   H. E. FRIES,   S. E. ALLEN,   R. D. BROWN.

On Finance.
J. M. ROGERS,   C. A. FOGLE,   W. B. CARTER, JR.

On Membership.
P. H. HANES,   H. E. FRIES,   R. J. REYNOLDS.

On Rooms.
W. A. WHITAKER,   C. A. HEGE,   R. J. REYNOLDS.

On Constitution.
J. W. FRIES,   W. A. WHITAKER,   G. W. HINSHAW.

Lucile Tobacco

W. A. WHITAKER, Proprietor.

Winston, N. C.

Among some of the popular brands of this well known manufactory are: "Lucile", "Golden Slipper", "Olive Branch", Twin-City, Marsh Mallow, White Wings, Billie Taylor, Dick Graves, Carrie Lee, Eldorado, Empress, Coronet, Long Tom, Peach and Honey, Royal Gold Bars, Sprig of Acacia, Twin-City Club, Sheila, Jefferson's Choice, Zip.

TWIST TOBACCOS.

Black Fat, Buzzard Wing, Falcon, Otto of Roses, White Wings.

SMOKING BRAND--WHITE WINGS.

These Tobaccos are made of the choicest leaf grown in the Piedmont belt which is unequalled in the world for its fine texture, delicacy of flavor and fine chewing quality, manufactured with great care and sold at bottom prices. If you want the best selling line of goods on the market write for samples and prices.

www.ingramcontent.com/pod-product-compliance
Lightning Source LLC
Chambersburg PA
CBHW020858160426
43192CB00007B/982